SpringerBriefs in Computer Science

More information about this series at http://www.springer.com/series/10028

Mohammed M. Alani

Elements of Cloud Computing Security

A Survey of Key Practicalities

 Springer

Mohammed M. Alani
Department of Information Technology
Al-Khawarizmi International College
Abu Dhabi
United Arab Emirates

ISSN 2191-5768   ISSN 2191-5776   (electronic)
SpringerBriefs in Computer Science
ISBN 978-3-319-41410-2   ISBN 978-3-319-41411-9   (eBook)
DOI 10.1007/978-3-319-41411-9

Library of Congress Control Number: 2016944339

Printed on acid-free paper

This Springer imprint is published by Springer Nature
The registered company is Springer International Publishing AG Switzerland

Foreword

Cloud computing has begun to revolutionize people lives, business, and services. The concept of cloud computing has emerged from virtualization and software design concepts. The emergence of service computing has revolutionized the software development methodologies. Cloud computing also offers different services (SaaS, PaaS, and IaaS) and deployment paradigms (private, public, and hybrid) that help business making relevant combinations that suit businesses and its impact on the global economy. In addition, there are also a number of advancements in the federation of clouds. However, challenges remain predominant to make cloud computing as a successful technology that will reach people and businesses. Such major challenges include cloud security, multitenancy, elasticity, secure and scalable service development and business sustainability.

This book has taken a major step in providing a breadth of knowledge on cloud security with elegance, examples, and comprehensive. This book has presented cloud security concepts in a simplified manner and elegant. Firstly, this book introduces the general concepts of cloud computing and then takes the reader very deeply into general concepts of cloud security techniques. This book has been well organized elegantly with five chapters.

Chapter 1 introduces the basic concepts and its underpinning technologies of cloud computing with simple illustration for all types of readers to understand. This chapter also explains the cloud's different service models and different deployment models. This chapter concludes with a discussion of cloud computing benefits to organizations.

Chapter 2 provides a brief introduction to cloud security. This chapter also discusses why cloud security is different from classical systems security.

Chapter 3 introduces to security threats in cloud computing very elegantly with detailed definitions of nine security threats such as data breaches, data loss, account or service hijacking, insecure interfaces and APIs, threats to availability, malicious insiders, abuse of cloud services, insufficient due diligence, and shared-technology vulnerabilities. In addition to the notorious nine, this chapter also explains additional threats such as lock-in, incomplete data deletion, and loss of governance among other threats along with their mitigation techniques.

Chapter 4 provides examples of cloud security attacks. A group of the most common attacks on the cloud was presented: denial-of-service attacks, hypervisor attacks, resource-freeing attacks, side-channel attacks, and attacks on confidentiality. This chapter also discusses mitigation techniques of those attacks.

Finally, Chap. 5 presents a short list of general security recommendations for the cloud adoption with emphasis given to good practice guidelines.

I am sure this book will make a huge impact on research as well as teaching and will add to a list of recommended books on cloud security. In light of the significant and fast emerging challenges that cloud computing face today, the author of this book has done an outstanding job in selecting the contents of this book. I am confident that this book will provide an appreciated contribution to the cloud computing and security community. It has the potential to become one of the main reference points for the years to come.

Leeds   Muthu Ramachandran
June 2016   www.soft-research.com

Preface

Network security is an ongoing effort full of challenges. It has become an integral part of any network service. With the rapidly increasing number of transactions happening on the Internet, security became a vital part of everyday life.

Network security becomes much more difficult to control when the environment becomes as dynamic and demanding as cloud computing.

Cloud computing aims at reducing costs. This reduction is not only in terms of computing resource, but also in terms of helping its users to focus on the business instead of the information technology enabling this business. Cloud computing has evolved from many different technologies such as virtualization, autonomic computing, grid computing, and many other technologies.

With every new technology, new challenges arise. A very important challenge is to provide adequate security to that cloud to perform as aimed.

This brief focuses on presenting cloud security concepts in a simplified way. After introducing the general concepts of cloud computing, the brief introduces the general concepts of cloud security by going through threats, attacks, and their mitigation techniques.

This brief starts by introducing the concepts and technologies underlying the cloud in Chap. 1. This chapter also explains the cloud's different service models and different deployment models. This chapter concludes with a discussion of cloud computing benefits to organizations.

Chapter 2 gives a brief introduction to cloud security. This chapter discusses why cloud security is different from classical systems security. This chapter also discusses the most famous cloud security incidents in the past few years.

Chapter 3 is devoted to security threats in cloud computing. This chapter discusses the nine most common security threats, referred to as the notorious nine: data breaches, data loss, account or service hijacking, insecure interfaces and APIs, threats to availability, malicious insiders, abuse of cloud services, insufficient due diligence, and shared-technology vulnerabilities. In addition to the notorious nine, this chapter also explains additional threats such as lock-in, incomplete data deletion, and loss of governance among other threats along with their mitigation techniques.

Security attacks on the cloud are discussed in Chap. 4. A group of the most common attacks on cloud was presented: denial-of-service attacks, hypervisor attacks, resource-freeing attacks, side-channel attacks, and attacks on confidentiality. This chapter also discusses mitigation techniques of those attacks.

Chapter 5 presents a short list of general security recommendations for the cloud.

Intended Audience of the Brief

- Researchers working in the cloud security field.
- Professionals in charge or involved in cloud computing.
- Graduate students.
- IT managers aiming to get basic understanding of cloud security challenges.

How to Use This Brief

If you are familiar with the general concepts of the cloud, its service models, and the underlying technologies, you can skip Chap. 1. If you have general knowledge about cloud security and how it is different from classic information security, you can skip Chap. 2 as well.

If you are new to the field of cloud computing, it is suggested that you start from Chap. 1 and go all the way up to Chap. 5.

Acknowledgments

Finally, I would like to thank my editors in Springer. You have made this project easy and simple. Thank you for believing in me. My final thanks go to my family, Marwa, little Aya and Mustafa, and mom and dad. Thank you all for enduring me during the time of working on this brief and all my life. I could not have been blessed more.

Abu Dhabi   Mohammed M. Alani
April 2016

Contents

1 What is the Cloud? 1
  1.1   Introduction 1
  1.2   History of Cloud Computing 2
  1.3   How Does the Cloud Work? 3
         1.3.1   Virtualization 3
         1.3.2   Clustering 5
         1.3.3   Grid Computing 6
         1.3.4   Cloud Architecture 7
         1.3.5   Cloud Operation 8
  1.4   Cloud Service Models 9
         1.4.1   Infrastructure-as-a-Service 9
         1.4.2   Platform-as-a-Service 10
         1.4.3   Software-as-a-Service 10
  1.5   Cloud Deployment Models 11
  1.6   Why Choose the Cloud? 12
  References 13

2 About Cloud Security 15
  2.1   Introduction 15
  2.2   Why Is Cloud Security Different? 17
  2.3   Famous Attacks on Cloud 18
         2.3.1   History of Denial of Service Attacks on the Cloud 18
         2.3.2   Other Attacks 20
  References 22

3 Security Threats in Cloud Computing 25
  3.1   Introduction 25
  3.2   Data Breaches 25
  3.3   Data Loss 27
  3.4   Account or Service Hijacking 28
  3.5   Insecure Interfaces and APIs 29
  3.6   Threats to Availability 30

3.7   Malicious Insiders   31
3.8   Abuse of Cloud Service   32
3.9   Insufficient Due Diligence.   33
3.10   Shared Technology Vulnerabilities.   34
3.11   Other Threats   35
References   37

4   **Security Attacks in Cloud Computing**.   41
4.1   Introduction   41
4.2   Denial of Service Attacks   41
4.3   Attacks on Hypervisor   44
4.4   Resource Freeing Attacks   45
4.5   Side-Channel Attacks.   46
4.6   Attacks on Confidentiality.   47
4.7   Other Attacks   48
References   48

5   **General Cloud Security Recommendations**   51
5.1   Introduction   51
5.2   General Security Recommendations   52
References   54

Index   55

Acronyms

ABE	Attribute-based encryption
API	Application programming interface
AWS	Amazon Web Services
DDoS	Distributed denial of service
DoS	Denial of service
EC2	Elastic Cloud Compute
FTP	File Transfer Protocol
HSVM	Hierarchical secure virtualization model
IaaS	Infrastructure-as-a-Service
IEEE	Institute of Electrical and Electronics Engineers
IP	Internet Protocol
LSM	Linux Security Module
MANET	Mobile ad hoc networks
NTP	Network Time Protocol
PaaS	Platform-as-a-Service
RFA	Resource-freeing attack
SaaS	Software-as-a-Service
SDN	Software-defined network
SETA	Security Educations, Training, and Awareness
SLA	Service Level Agreement
URL	Uniform Resource Locator
VM	Virtual machine
VPS	Virtual private server
VoIP	Voice-over Internet Protocol
WWW	World Wide Web

Chapter 1
What is the Cloud?

Abstract This chapter provides a simplified introduction to cloud computing. This chapter starts by introducing the history of cloud computing and moves on to describe the cloud architecture and operation. This chapter also discusses briefly cloud service models: Infrastructure-as-a-Service, Platform-as-a-Service, and Software-as-a-Service. Clouds are also categorized based on their ownership to private and public clouds. This chapter concludes by explaining the reasons for choosing cloud computing over other technologies by exploring the economic and technological benefits of the cloud.

Keywords Cloud computing · IaaS · PaaS · SaaS · Private cloud · Public cloud

1.1 Introduction

The main purpose of creating networks is, simply, sharing resources. These resources can be files, photographs, printers, space on a hard disk, or a music file we would like to listen together. Networks have helped us become more connected with everything and everyone around us. Currently, networks provide us with many services including the World Wide Web (WWW), electronic mail, voice over-internet-protocol (VoIP), instant messaging, and many other services.

Network services usually fall into one of two models: peer to peer and client–server. In a *peer-to-peer* network service, computers can communicate directly without the need to be connected all the time nor the need to have an always-on server to supervise the process. In *client–server* model, one device acts as a client that requests a service from another device called the server. The server needs to be always on and always connected and waits for client requests.

So many services on the Internet, and even on local networks, operate based on a client–server model. For example, to view a webpage using WWW service, a client sends a request to view a specific webpage identified by a Uniform Resource Locator (URL) to a server, namely a web server. The server is just sitting there waiting for client requests. When you check your e-mail, the software that you use, like Outlook, or Thunderbird, acts as a client and asks the e-mail server to send information about

© The Author(s) 2016
M.M. Alani, *Elements of Cloud Computing Security*,
SpringerBriefs in Computer Science, DOI 10.1007/978-3-319-41411-9_1

new messages. Even services that operates on the peer-to-peer model, like voice chat, rely partially on client–server model. Most voice chat services work in the following sequence:

1. Your client software connects to a server and registers your IP address.
2. The other side's client software connects to the same server to register its IP address.
3. When you want to make a voice call to the other side, your client software contacts the server to check whether the other side is online, and if it is online, what is its IP address.
4. Your client software initiates a voice call to the other client directly.

As you can see, the actual peer-to-peer communication occurred only at Step 4, while the first three steps were all client–server activities. What we want to conclude from this explanation is that client–server model is essential in most network services we use in our daily life. Servers are an essential part of the client–server model. That is basically why we are studying cloud computing.

When an organization works on setting up a network service, an essential part of the preparation is to select a suitable server. The organization chooses the hardware specifications based on the application requirements. In addition to the server hardware, there are other components that need to be provided to host the network service successfully including security, Internet connectivity, and backup electricity. The IT manager, wanting to get rid of all of this responsibility of keeping the service up and running all the time, suggests that the organization should outsource hosting the network service. This would push the burden of managing the server availability and security to another organization. Three possible scenarios are available now: shared hosting, Virtual Private Server (VPS), and dedicated servers.

Shared hosting is out of the question if the network service requires any server control and it is more than just a simple website with a limited number of visitors. The second solution is which is renting a dedicated server. Dedicated servers are physical servers with specifications selected by the client (most of the time). These servers are hosted by a service provider that provides all the necessary support like Internet connection, firewall, and sometimes off-line backup. Usually, these dedicated servers are very costly as compared to VPSs. VPS can be an economic solution where a service provider uses a physical server with high specifications to host a group of logical servers and rent those servers (for a monthly or annual fee) to client individuals or organizations. This can be a suitable solution if your network service does not require a lot of processing power and the number of users is limited.

1.2 History of Cloud Computing

The general concept of cloud computing, although it was holding a different name, goes back to 1961 [1]. A well-known computer scientist named John McCarthy stated, at the MIT Centennial *"computers of the kind I have advocated become the computers of the future, then computing may someday be organized as a public utility just as the telephone system is a public utility... The computer utility could become the basis of a new and important industry."*

The term *utility computing* refers to a computer-on-demand service that can be used by the public with a pay-for-what-you-use financial model. The term has been evolving since then.

The idea was slightly matured before the end of the 1990s when Salesforce.com introduced the first remotely provisioned service to the enterprise. Afterward, the concept started being different near the end of the 1990s. The concepts then focused on an abstraction layer used to facilitate data delivery methods in packet-switched heterogeneous networks.

In 2002, Amazon.com introduced Amazon Web Services (AWS) platform. The platform, back then, provided remotely provisioned computing resources and storage.

Commercially, the term "cloud computing" emerged in 2006 when Amazon launched its Elastic Compute Cloud (EC2) services. The service model was based on "leasing" elastic computing processing power and storage where enterprises can run their apps. Later that year, Google also started providing Google Apps.

Cloud computing was identified by NIST in [2] as

"a model for enabling ubiquitous, convenient, on-demand network access to a shared pool of configurable computing resources (e.g., networks, servers, storage, applications, and services) that can be rapidly provisioned and released with minimal management effort or service provider interaction."

We can identify the Internet as a network of networks from all around the world. Since, in the broad sense, the cloud uses the Internet as a provisioning medium, the term "cloud" comes as a metaphor for the Internet itself. A better understanding of the history of cloud computing can be understood by knowing the combination of technologies that had evolved into the cloud. The next section will discuss those technologies briefly.

1.3 How Does the Cloud Work?

Cloud computing is the result of interaction between many disciplines in computer science. Before we explain how cloud computing works, we will go through some basic definitions of underlying technologies.

1.3.1 Virtualization

As an important enabling technology to cloud computing, we need to explain the concept of virtualization before we proceed. A virtual computer, as identified in [3], is

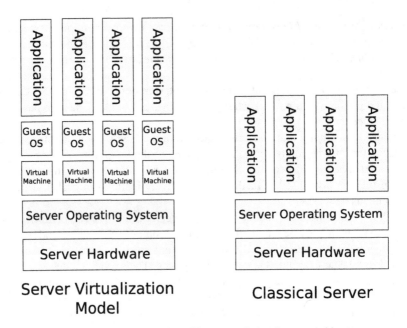

Fig. 1.1 Comparison of traditional server architecture and virtual server architecture

"a logical representation of a computer in software. By decoupling the physical hardware from the operating system, virtualization provides more operational flexibility and increases the utilization rate of the underlying physical hardware."

Figure 1.1 shows a comparison between a traditional server model and a virtual server model. In this figure, you can see that the traditional server has one operating system and multiple applications installed on it. On the other side, you see the virtualized server model where the physical server holds a host operating system that is hosting multiple virtual machines. Each virtual machine has its own guest operating system and application(s).

Virtualization was previously supported by software only. However, currently, most new processors support virtualization in hardware. There can be many discussions of how deep virtualization can go and whether full isolation of the guest operating system is done or there might be a degree of kernel sharing between the host operating system and the guest operating system. However, these details are beyond the scope of this book. To understand how virtualization helps in improving utilization of resource, we will look at an example. In the example, four different organizations, namely A, B, C, and D, are using their own servers hosted within their premises. The servers are designed to provide a certain network service, like web hosting of the organization's website. These organizations are medium-sized and their servers are not fully loaded. In fact, some of those servers are lightly loaded most of the time. In Fig. 1.2a, you can see how those servers are underutilized. Figure 1.2b shows how using one hardware server with higher processing power as a

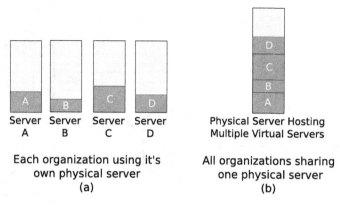

Fig. 1.2 Individual physical server utilization versus virtualized server utilization

virtualization host can result in the creation of one virtual machine for each organization. This will result in cost saving, both in capital expenditures and in operational expenditures, and much better resource utilization.

1.3.2 Clustering

Clustering is the grouping of interconnected independent resources working as a single system. Clustering provides high reliability and availability due to the existence of other resources that can cover the need. In order to create a properly working cluster, it is advised that servers that form the cluster have identical hardware [1]. This would guarantee identical performance levels among the servers forming the cluster.

As shown in Fig. 1.3, clustering techniques are based on having a front-end dispatcher that receives the requests from clients and forwards it to the cluster servers. The dispatcher holds an IP address that is usually referred to as the *cluster address*. Beyond that cluster address, there is a group of servers operating at the back-end to provide the actual service. The client sees only the cluster address and does not see the rest of the cluster. This is how client transparency is achieved. On the other hand, in many cases, you set up the servers inside the cluster as independent servers operating a certain network service and the dispatcher distributing jobs between them. This is how you can achieve server transparency as well. This setup will save a lot of time and effort trying to maintain servers' consistency if the clustering was not server transparent [4].

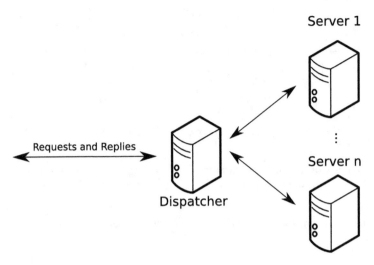

Fig. 1.3 Clustering

1.3.3 Grid Computing

A *computing grid* is a group of servers that work together to achieve a certain goal without the need to be in the same physical location nor the need to have identical specifications. The sole requirement of the grid is to have servers connected together using a communications network. The servers connected as a grid can be temporarily connected just long enough to achieve the common goal [5].

The principal components of the grid can be listed as follows:

1. Networks
2. Computational nodes (servers)
3. Grid middleware
4. Grid applications

Since we are talking about servers that do not reside in the same location, the efficiency of the networks linking those servers is a deciding factor in how efficient the grid can be. If you connect those servers using a slow or unreliable network, you cannot make use of the grid. The servers, as stated earlier, do not need to be similar in hardware specifications. Its also even possible to connect servers that use different operating systems. Those servers must be able to run a grid-specific middleware that allows grid components to interact properly and communicate effectively. On top of that middleware, grid applications run. The applications running on a grid must be written specifically for the grid computing model to harvest the benefits of grid computing [6]. Figure 1.4 shows the layers of the grid.

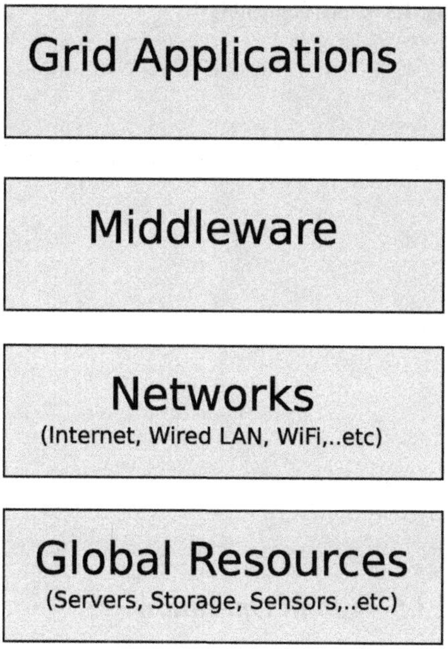

Fig. 1.4 Layers of grid computing

1.3.4 Cloud Architecture

In general, the conceptual architecture of the cloud is shown in Fig. 1.5. The figure shows how the cloud is based on multiple physical servers operating together as a single unit. The lowest layer contains the servers' hardware like processors, memory modules, and storage. Over the hardware layer lies an abstraction layer. The abstraction layer, as you see in the figure, extends over multiple physical machines. This abstraction layer is the one responsible for dynamically creating virtual machines and controlling where and how these virtual machines operate. In many cases, you will find that the host operating system is mixed with the abstraction layer. This happens when we use cloud-dedicated operating systems like Eucalyptus [7]. Usually, the cloud servers' hardware and the abstraction layer are referred to as the *cloud infrastructure*.

Three more layers exist over the abstraction layer: Infrastructure-as-a-Service (IaaS), Platform-as-a-Service(PaaS), and Software-as-a-Service(SaaS). Each one of those layers represents a service model of the cloud. These service models will be discussed in the upcoming subsections. We cannot conclude cloud architecture without introducing the term "hypervisor." The *hypervisor* is the software, firmware, or hardware that creates and runs virtual machines. In Fig. 1.5, the hypervisor operates at the abstraction layer. Many commercial examples of hypervisors like Xen, KVM, Virtual Box, and VMware ESX/ESXi exist.

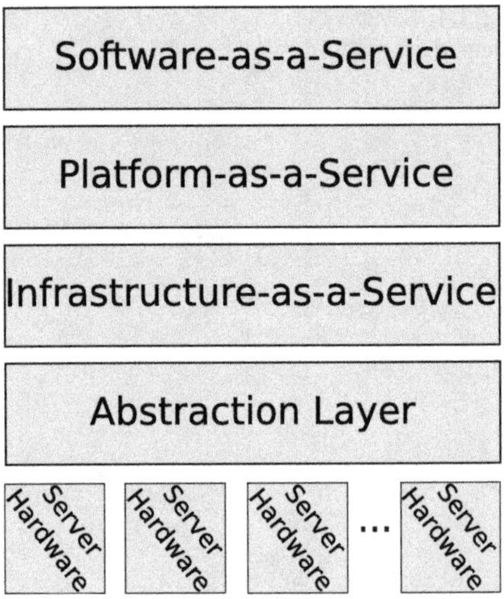

Fig. 1.5 Cloud computing
layers

1.3.5   Cloud Operation

To have a better understanding of how we moved from the stand-alone server era to the cloud era, we will explain it through an example. Our example is a college registration system. This system is web-based, and students use it to register for classes every semester. As a web administrator, you have to choose a proper server that would have adequate processing power to server the 11,000 students of the college. You do your calculations and assume that 500 students will be using the system at the same time. You end up asking your IT manager for three servers with 64 GB of RAM, 4 TB of SSD hard disk, and 8 processors each. You explain to the IT manager that these high specifications will help in providing the service in an acceptable quality. After a couple of fights over the annual budget, the IT manager accepts the fact that this is a necessity and cuts the 30,000$ off the IT budget. You install your web application before the fall semester registration period, and all students are very happy with the service and happy with the fact that they can register for their classes at home. Two weeks later, the registration period is over. The 30,000$ servers are useless until the next semester. You start thinking about the rough truth that these servers will be used for 6 weeks every year. They will be almost idle for the other 46 weeks of the year. What are the possible solutions? The answer is an on-demand computing service that can provide you with processing power and storage only when needed: cloud computing.

Now, the question is, how will the cloud handle the registration system of the college?

The college will subscribe to a cloud service provided by a cloud service provider. The IT staff will set up the first virtual machine and install the necessary registration application on it. The virtual machine will remain available waiting for user requests. When the registration period starts, the cloud will fire up. Whenever the virtual machine is almost fully loaded, the abstraction layer generates another virtual machine to handle the increasing load. If both of them become almost fully loaded, another virtual machine is generated and so on. The capacity allocated to the college registration system will be elastic. This capacity, whether in one virtual machine or multiple, will be increased by the cloud automatically whenever a need is felt. When the load starts to lighten up, the additional (idle) virtual machines are removed. In this scenario, the college will be paying for the resources they use only. There will not be underutilized nor overloaded servers.

1.4 Cloud Service Models

As we have mentioned in the previous section, the cloud comes in three possible service models: IaaS, PaaS, and SaaS. These three levels basically identify the level of involvement of the client in the server provisioning process. The higher you go in Fig. 1.5, the less involved the client needs to be and the higher the cost becomes. Whenever you give more work to the service provider, the cost meter tends to go up.

1.4.1 Infrastructure-as-a-Service

IaaS model is the lowest level of service provided to the client. In this service model, the cloud computing client is provided with a controlled access to the virtual infrastructure. Using this access, the client can install operating system and application software. From the client's point of view, this model is similar to renting the hardware from a service provider and letting the service provider manage the hardware. In this sense, the client does not have control over the physical hardware. On the other hand, the client will have to manage the security aspects from the operating system and up to the applications. This model requires the client to have highly experienced network engineer(s). Handling everything from the operating system and up is a big responsibility that most clients decline to handle, especially because of the security burdens. Thus, this model is not of high preference in the cloud computing clients' society [8].

The IaaS's virtual infrastructure is provisioned on demand using an Application Programming Interface (API) or a web interface. In summary, IaaS takes away the burden of procurement and maintenance of hardware and pushes it over to the cloud service provider side.

IaaS is identified by NIST as

"The capability provided to the consumer is to provision processing, storage, networks, and other fundamental computing resources where the consumer is able to deploy and run arbitrary software, which can include operating systems and applications. The consumer does not manage or control the underlying cloud infrastructure

but has control over operating systems, storage, and deployed applications; and possibly limited control of select networking components (e.g., host firewalls)" [2].

1.4.2   Platform-as-a-Service

In PaaS, the operating system and all platform-related tools (like compilers) are already installed for the client. These preinstalled components are also managed by the cloud service provider.

Clients have the freedom of installing additional tools based on their needs. However, the control over the infrastructure is retained by the service provider. The client controls application development, configuration, and deployment. In some aspects, this service model is similar to the traditional web-hosting services in which clients rent a remote server with development platform preinstalled on it. The major difference between this model and traditional web-hosting is the rapid provisioning. Traditional web-hosting is managed manually and requires human intervention when the demand increases or decreases. On the other hand, provisioning in cloud computing is automatic and rapid. Thus, it does not require any human interventions [8].

PaaS is identified by NIST as

"The capability provided to the consumer is to deploy onto the cloud infrastructure consumer-created or acquired applications created using programming languages, libraries, services, and tools supported by the provider. The consumer does not manage or control the underlying cloud infrastructure including network, servers, operating systems, or storage, but has control over the deployed applications and possibly configuration settings for the application-hosting environment" [2].

1.4.3   Software-as-a-Service

SaaS model focuses on the application level and abstracts the user away from infrastructure and platform details. Usually, applications are provisioned via thin client interfaces such as web browsers or even mobile phone apps [8]. Microsoft Outlook.com is a clear example of this. An organization can adopt Outlook.com electronic mail service and never bother about hardware maintenance, service uptime, security, or even operating system management. The client is given the control over certain parameters in the software configuration, for example, creating and deleting mail boxes. These parameters can be controlled through the interface of the application.

This service model gives the client the luxury of not worrying about hardware, operating system, host security, patching, and updating,...etc. Instead, the client will be able to focus on using the application and achieving business goals.

SaaS is identified by NIST as

"The capability provided to the consumer is to use the providers applications running on a cloud infrastructure 2. The applications are accessible from various client devices through either a thin client interface, such as a web browser (e.g., web-based e-mail), or a program interface. The consumer does not manage or control the underlying cloud infrastructure including network, servers, operating systems, storage, or even individual application capabilities, with the possible exception of limited user-specific application configuration settings" [2].

1.5 Cloud Deployment Models

In addition to service models presented earlier, we need to look at deployment models as well. The two main deployment models are public and private clouds. A *public cloud* can be identified as a cloud service provided to the general public. A public cloud can be owned and managed by a cloud service provider (such as Google and Microsoft), academic institution, or the government. This cloud can provide services to multiple clients and its usually hosted at the premises of the cloud service provider.

The public cloud can be either dedicated or shared. The dedicated public cloud provides cloud services on a dedicated physical infrastructure in which the cloud service provider is responsible for architecture, customization, and security (on infrastructure level not application level). In a shared public cloud, which is the most common deployment model, the physical infrastructure is shared by multiple clients. In this submodel, the service provider is also responsible for architecture, customization, and infrastructure security.

On the other hand, a *private cloud* can be identified as a cloud service used by a single organization or its multiple business units. This cloud can be owned and managed by the organization itself, a cloud service provider, or a mixture of both. This type of cloud can be hosted on organization premises or somewhere else. Many organizations prefer private clouds so that they can maintain control over service delivery environment. For example, banks and governmental institutions have very strict security requirements that they cannot leave to the cloud service provider.

Private clouds can be self-hosted, hosted, or private cloud appliance.

In self-hosted private cloud, the physical resources reside at the owner organization's premises and the whole cloud solution is designed, hosted, and managed by the owner organization. In a hosted private cloud, the cloud solution is designed by the organization while hosted and managed by another organization. This type of private cloud mixes the benefits of full control over the cloud with the benefits of data center outsourcing. In a private cloud appliance, the cloud environment is designed by a vendor or a service provider and hosted internally in the organization. The management can be done either internally or externally. This model lowers the deployment risk since the solution is designed by a vendor that has the technical capability to create a secure design.

Two other, less popular, types of cloud exist: hybrid cloud and community cloud. A *community cloud* is a cloud infrastructure deployed to be used by a specific community of client organizations that have shared interests. This cloud can be owned, managed, and operated by one or more of the organizations in the community, a third party, or some combination of them, and it may exist on or off premises [8].

A *hybrid cloud* is a mix of two or more cloud infrastructures (public, private, and community) that are tied together using technologies that enable application and data portability [2].

1.6 Why Choose the Cloud?

The general benefits of using the cloud can be summarized in the following points:

1. **Cost Saving.**
   When you use the cloud instead of the classical server model, you will be saving in many ways. The first component of cost saving would be the reduction in capital expenditure. The organization will not have to pay for server(s) hardware. Another component of saving is saving in the operational expenditure of the classical servers. Costs previously spent on Internet connectivity, electricity, maintenance, and hardware depreciation will be eliminated. However, the operational expenditure for cloud computing is not cheap as compared to the operational expenditure of classical server model.
   In general, cloud computing is an on-demand service. This means that under-utilization of resources will be cut down to the minimum. If we go back to the example explained earlier in this section, the college registration system is an excellent candidate to use cloud computing instead of classic server model. The college will not need to spend 30,000$ on server hardware.
2. **Scalability and Flexibility**.
   The elastic nature of the cloud makes it suitable for handling increasing amounts of traffic. Sudden increase in the processing, or storage, requirements, and gradual increases can easily be handled by the cloud by generating more VMs on the fly. This unique feature in the cloud makes it a very suitable candidate for many network services. The fact that resources are available on demand and removed when not needed makes the cloud one of the most economic solutions for organizations looking for outsources hosting of their networking services.
   The scalability provided by the cloud can be divided into two types: horizontal and vertical. *Horizontal scaling* is the process of allocating or releasing resources of the same type. For example, creating a new virtual machine with the same capabilities of the current virtual machine to enable the system to handle more load is horizontal scaling. On the other hand, *vertical scaling* is the process of replacing a resource with another resource of higher or lower capacity, for example, replacing a virtual machine with 8 processor cores with the one of 4 processor

cores only [1]. Most of the time, vertical scaling requires certain settings, while horizontal scaling can be done by automatically replicating resources.

3. **Reliability**.

   As the cloud is formed by a number of physical servers, reliability comes from the fact that if one physical machine fails, other physical machines can handle the load dynamically such that the failure is invisible to regular users.

4. **Reduced Management Efforts**.

   Whether your organization is using a private cloud or a public cloud, or even a hybrid, the efforts exercised by the IT team are less as compared to classic server architecture. The dynamic nature of the cloud allows it to stretch to handle the additional load automatically without the need of human interference. The same dynamic nature allows the cloud to handle hardware failures with much needed flexibility. The organization's IT team does not need to panic whenever a memory module fails in a server because the other servers will handle the load while the failed machine is being fixed.

5. **Reduced Environmental Effect**.

   Whenever you are sharing the hardware resource, you are saving the environment by reducing the amounts of carbon footprint. Since one of the main aims of cloud computing is to provide better utilization of hardware resource, the cloud will cause reduction in the 7.8 billion tons of CO_2 emitted per year [9].

6. **Better Hardware Resources Utilization.**

   This point can be easily understood by looking at Fig. 1.2. Although the figure shows the utilization of virtualization, the same exact concept is valid for cloud computing. Instead of having four physical servers utilized between 10 and 20 %, it is possible to use one physical server with higher capacity to host all the other servers as virtual machines. The host server, in this case, would have a much higher utilization.

Other benefits such as the ease of capacity planning, organizational agility, reduction in IT technical overhead, and collaboration efficiency.

About a decade ago, whenever someone thinks about creating a network service, he/she thinks about the hardware specifications of the server taking into consideration expected number of users, expected network traffic, expected growth, and so many other things that take a lot of time and effort to figure out, and most of the time, these servers are underutilized or overloaded. With the existence of cloud computing, you need to worry about developing your application rather than the "logistics" of delivering this application to the public.

References

1. T. Erl, R. Puttini, Z. Mahmood, *Cloud Computing: Concepts, Technology & Architecture* (Pearson Education, USA, 2013)
2. P. Mell, T. Grance, The nist definition of cloud computing (2011)
3. I.G. Education, Virtualization in education. IBM Corporation, Whitepaper (2007)

4. T. Schroeder, S. Goddard, B. Ramamurthy, Scalable web server clustering technologies. Netw. IEEE **14**(3), 38–45 (2000)
5. F. Berman, G. Fox, A.J.G. Hey, *Grid Computing: Making the Global Infrastructure a Reality* (Wiley, New York, 2003)
6. F. Berman, G. Fox, A.J. Hey, *Grid Computing: Making the Global Infrastructure a Reality*, vol. 2 (Wiley, New York, 2003)
7. D. Nurmi, R. Wolski, C. Grzegorczyk, G. Obertelli, S. Soman, L. Youseff, D. Zagorodnov, The eucalyptus open-source cloud-computing system, in *9th IEEE/ACM International Symposium on Cluster Computing and the Grid, 2009. CCGRID'09* (IEEE, New York, 2009), pp. 124–131
8. R. Hill, L. Hirsch, P. Lake, S. Moshiri, *Guide to Cloud Computing: Principles and Practice* (Springer Science & Business Media, London, 2012)
9. S.K. Garg, R. Buyya, Green cloud computing and environmental sustainability, in *Harnessing Green IT: Principles and Practices* (Wiley, UK, 2012), pp. 315–340

Chapter 2
About Cloud Security

Abstract This chapter starts by discussing how cloud computing security is different from classical network security. The chapter mentions some threats and attacks that apply specifically to cloud computing. The chapter elaborates on most recent real-life attacks to cloud computing in the past few years. The chapter also explains the history of Denial of Service attacks along with other attacks.

Keywords Cloud computing · Iaas · Paas · Saas · Security · Cloud security

2.1 Introduction

As our lives become more and more connected, network security becomes more and more challenging. Security has become an integral part of any network service. With the rapidly increasing number of transactions happening on the Internet, security has become an essential part of everyday life.

The context of network security becomes much more difficult to control when the environment becomes as dynamic and demanding as cloud computing.

The main aim of cloud computing is cost reduction and efficiency improvement. This cost reduction is not only in terms of computing resources, but also in terms of helping its users to focus on the business instead of the information technology enabling this business. Cloud computing is the result of developments in many technology directions such as virtualization, autonomic-computing, grid-computing, and many other technologies as explained earlier in Chap. 1.

As always, with every new technology, new challenges arise. A very important challenge is providing adequate security to that cloud to perform in alliance with business objectives.

After discussing the basics of cloud computing in Chap. 1, in this chapter we will focus on basic security aspects. At the start of our discussion, we must be familiar with three basic concepts: vulnerability, threats, and attack. In the Internet Engineering Task Force (IETF) RFC 2828 [1], a *vulnerability* is defined as a flaw or weakness in a system's design, implementation, or operation and management that could be exploited to violate the system's security policy. A *threat* is identified as a potential

M.M. Alani, *Elements of Cloud Computing Security*,
SpringerBriefs in Computer Science, DOI 10.1007/978-3-319-41411-9_2

for violation of security, which exists when there is a circumstance, capability, action, or event that could breach security and cause harm. On the other hand, the same RFC identifies an *attack* as an assault on system security that derives from an intelligent threat, i.e., an intelligent act that is a deliberate attempt to evade security services and violate the security policy of a system.

In general, computer security identifies three main objectives:

- Confidentiality: Assuring that data are available only to eligible entities and no unauthorized access to data can be obtained.
- Integrity: Assuring that data have not been altered in any way while it is stored or while its transport over the network.
- Authentication: Assuring the identity of the entity involved in the communication.

However, with the emergence of new technologies and threats, two more objectives can be added to the previous list:

- Availability: Assuring that data and services are always available at the required time.
- Accountability: Assuring that no entity can deny its participation in a data transfer between them.

These security objectives require the employment of certain security mechanisms and services to be implemented. We can identify a security mechanism as a process, or a device, aimed to detect, prevent, or recover from a security attack. Security mechanisms like encryption, hashing, steganography, etc. are commonly used in achieving security objectives.

A *security service* can be identified as a processing or communication service aimed to enhance the security of data and the information transfers of an entity. These services help in countering security attacks. Security services usually employ one or more security mechanism to achieve its goals [2].

While computer security is an important concept, network security remains a broader sense. Network security focuses on prevention of unauthorized access to data, software, and hardware at the network level, rather than on host level. It is the proactive detection of active attacks against the resources, the prevention of unnecessary security vulnerabilities, and rapid, appropriate response when a security event takes place. In general, network security consists of three layers: border security, authentication, and authorization. Border security focuses mostly on network layer security devices such as firewalls, intrusion detection systems, and intrusion prevention systems. Authentication helps in assuring identities of users as explained above, while *authorization* is identifying which resources an authenticated users can access, and which type of access this user is granted.

2.2 Why Is Cloud Security Different?

As with any other system, cloud computing includes vulnerabilities. These vulnerabilities, when exploited by attackers, can cause service disruptions, data loss, data theft, etc. Given the nature of dynamic resource sharing that take place in the cloud, it is possible that classical attacks and vulnerabilities can cause more harm on a cloud system if it is not protected properly.

The context in which network security can be discussed can identify a long list of threats and attacks. However, the dynamic and unique nature of the cloud can require additional measures and this nature also opens the door for a whole new list of attacks that can be used against the cloud.

Nothing explains this better than an example. One of the unique characteristics of the cloud is availability. The cloud is designed to be available all the time. Whether it is a private or a public cloud, availability is an undeniable feature that many organizations seek. What if attackers target availability of the cloud?

One of the major reasons why organizations decide to switch to a cloud environment is the you-pay-for-what-you-use business model. No one likes paying for resource that are not very well utilized. Hence, when an attack such as Denial-of-Service (DoS) attack happens, not only availability is targeted.

Denial of Service (DoS) attacks aim at making a certain network service unavailable to its legitimate users. In its basic form, these attacks keep the resources busy such that these resources become unavailable to the users this service was aimed to serve.

Using DoS attacks on the cloud, the attacker can cause huge financial implications by consuming high resources in the trial of making the service unavailable. So, for the organization using the cloud, it is a doubled loss.

The organization will be paying a lot of money for the resources consumed by the attack and, after a while, the organization's service will be unavailable due to the DoS attack. This type of attacks is referred to as Fraudulent Resource Consumption (FRC) [3].

The previous example shows us how the same attack can have different effect on different technology. For example, DoS attack on a classic server would render the service unavailable. If the same attack happens on a mobile ad hoc network, it would make the service unavailable and consume valuable battery life [4]. On the other hand, DoS on the cloud would render the service unavailable and cost the organization a lot of money for the consumed resources. This is why the uniqueness of the cloud technology open the door for unique attacks or at least unique effects of old common attacks.

Having the multiple layers discussed in Chap. 1, cloud computing can be target for attacks at any of these levels. We will see in the coming chapters that threats exist at virtually any lever of the cloud computing system. As you will see, there are threats at the hypervisor level, threats at the platform level, threats at the software level, etc. All of these attacks are unique to cloud computing alone and cannot be used on classical network security model.

Given the dynamic nature and the huge processing power of the cloud, it can also be used by attackers as a powerful attacking tool. The attacker can benefit from the on-demand processing power and employ it in performing DoS attacks among other attacking choices.

2.3 Famous Attacks on Cloud

Although cloud computing, in its current definition, is not that old, the cloud has got its good share of attacks.

2.3.1 History of Denial of Service Attacks on the Cloud

With rapidly increasing applications on the Internet, people rely more and more on Internet-based services in their regular daily actions. Availability of these services has grown to be one of the biggest concerns for both clients and service providers. During the past few years, many attacks have targeted availability of Internet-based services. As network security research grew stronger, simple DoS attacks were not as important as they were once. DoS attacks became less effective and easily detectable. Since the regular DoS attack comes from a single source, it becomes less effective once the source is detected by security appliances, or software, and blocked. A more sophisticated and harder to detect version evolved, namely Distributed Denial of Service (DDoS) attack.

A *DDoS attack* is an attack that targets availability of a system and is launched from multiple locations at the same time. The idea behind launching the attack from multiple location is to make detection much harder. Figure 2.1 shows how a DDoS attack works.

Figure 2.1 shows how an attacker implants malicious code in computers or servers that are not well protected. At the attack time, the attacker gives orders to the bots to

Fig. 2.1 Anatomy of DDoS attack

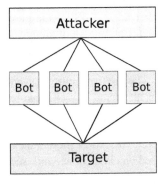

start the attacks. Sometimes even giving orders is not necessary as malicious codes can work based on a specific action time preprogrammed. Usually, after the attack, the attacker cleans up all log files and other traces that can lead back to him/her. This would make it nearly impossible to trace back the source of the attack.

As explained earlier, in DDoS attacks, a DoS attack is launched from multiple sources, usually tens or hundreds, at the same time. Because it is coming from multiple source, DDoS attack is harder to detect and deter as compared to simple DoS attacks.

Reports show that only six DDoS attacks took place in the year 1988. The year 2000 witnessed DDoS attacks on large websites such as CNN, Yahoo, and Amazon. At that time, reports shown that DDoS attack rates reached 1 GBps.

In 2007, DDoS attacks reached the rates of 70 GBps. In 2013, a huge attack took place on Spamhaus spam detection service that reached the huge rate of 300 GBps. This attack aimed at bringing down Spamhaus so that the blacklisted sources of spam can go undetected on the Internet.

In February 2014, the largest DDoS attack in history took place with the rate of 400 GBps which is the largest known DDoS attack known until now.

The largest DDoS attack in history mentioned earlier targeted a public cloud service provider called CloudFlare. Attacks of such magnitude affect not only their targets, but affect the overall Internet in the area. Regular Internet users experienced noticeable slowness in their Internet services around the world that day.

DDoS attacks can launched in many different mechanisms. However, the purpose is the same, prevent the legitimate users from using the system. DDoS can be done through flooding, amplification, malformed packets, or exploiting a vulnerability in a networking protocol [5]. The mechanism of attack used against CloudFlare was Network Time Protocol (NTP) amplification.

NTP is a simple protocol that helps computers set their time accurately by contacting an NTP server. NTP protocol uses UDP at the transport layer, which means that it does not require any handshake, nor acknowledgment like TCP [6]. The attack uses a very old attacking technique called spoofing. *IP address spoofing* is sending an IP packet with a fake source IP address.

The attacker starts the NTP amplification attack using a rogue NTP server that is controlled by the attacker on an network that does not prevent spoofing. A large number of UDP segments with spoofed source IP address putting the target's IP address as the source of all of those packets. The spoofed packets are directed to a large number of NTP servers (on standard NTP port 123). These requests are not sent using simple NTP commands rather using MONLIST command. MONLIST command, in NTP, results in a response around 206 times the request size. The command MONLIST sends a list of upto the last 600 IP addresses that last accessed the NTP server [7]. In theory, an attacker with 1 Gbps link can generate more than 200 Gbps of DDoS traffic.

According to details published by CloudFlare in [8], the attacker(s) used 4,529 NTP servers running on 1,298 different networks. On average, each server sent around 87 Mbps of DDoS traffic to CloudFlare's network. Again, in theory, the attacker could have used a single attacking server to start the attack. All the attacker needed was a network that does not prevent spoofing to initiate the requests.

NTP amplification seem to be much more dangerous as compared to DNS amplification attacks the were used to attack Spamhaus in 2013. The attacker needed about 1/7th the number of compromised servers that were used in the Spamhaus attack, yet produced 33 % more traffic.

The dynamic nature of cloud computing can be beneficial to counter DDoS attacks in some scenarios. However, the different levels at which DDoS attacks can be performed on a cloud-based service can make defense more complex, as we will see in the next chapters.

2.3.2 Other Attacks

Amazon provides a user interface for its clients through which the clients can start new instances of a machine, terminating an instance among other control actions. In 2008, a vulnerability was found in this control service. The vulnerability was about using a special type of Signature Wrapping Attack, the attacker would be able to modify an eavesdropped message despite the digital signature of the message. Through this modification, the attacker would be able to execute any code they want on the server machine. This attack can be split into two separate activities; attacking the cloud control interface to get control of the cloud system, then attacking the service instances using the service-to-cloud attack surface [9]. In 2011, the year of cloud data breaches, the website TripAdvisor, which was hosted on the cloud, was compromised and users e-mail addresses were stolen. The attack is thought to be a possible SQL-injection type of attack [10].

In 2015, a security vulnerability named venom was detected in many cloud-based data centers. This vulnerability can allow hackers to take over entire data centers, presumably even those owned by Amazon, RackSpace, and Oracle. Venom stands for Virtualized Environment Neglected Operations Manipulation.

Another massive breach that took place in 2011 was Sony attacks. Sony had around a dozen data breaches in 2011 that hit its Sony PlayStation Network, Sony Pictures, Sony Online Entertainment, along a few other Sony-owned websites. The attacks compromised around 100 million user accounts. The compromise included password and other private data. Given the frequency of password reuse by users, there is a very good probability that user account in other online services can be targeted using the obtained information form Sony breaches. In this attack, attackers gained access to one server that was not well protected and started escalating from there to obtain access to many other servers. Sony's network was not layered well enough to isolate breaches happening in one part of the network to proceed to the rest of the network. The clear weakness in Sony's security was evident when the attackers published server certificates that used the password "password." These certificates were later used to distribute malware. Many weaknesses contributed to the Sony breach including the use of weak passwords, lack of individual server hardening, lack of proper network isolation, not having proper security controls to set off alerts, not responding to alerts properly, in adequate logging and monitoring, and lack of security awareness [11, 12].

In 2011 as well, attackers targeted a cloud-based Nasdaq system named "Directors Desk." The system facilitates communication between 10,000 senior executives and company directors. By having access to this system, attacks can eavesdrop on private conversations between executives that can be used as stock market-leaked information to benefit competitors. While attackers had not directly attacked trading servers, they were able to install malware on sensitive systems, which enabled them to spy on dozens of company directors. This kind of attack has a long-term effect that cannot be easily calculated now [13].

Another attack that happened in 2011 was the Epsilon attack. Epsilon is a cloud-based e-mail service provider that went under attack in April, 2011. The attack was a spear phishing attack. While a *phishing* attack is a type of social engineering attack in which attackers use spoofed e-mail messages to trick victims into sharing sensitive information or installing malware on their computers, spear phishing is a more complex type of phishing. Spear phishing attacks use specific knowledge of individuals and their organizations to make the spoofed e-mail look more legitimate and targeted to a specific person [14]. In the attack on Epsilon, data of 75 business organizations were beached and the list was growing. Although Epsilon did not disclose the names of companies affected by the attack, it is estimated that around 60 million customer e-mails were breached.

A few other cloud-based breaches happened in 2011. This have slowed down the pace of adoption of the cloud by businesses in the next year. However, cloud adoption recovered from these breaches because most of these breaches were not cloud specific and could have happened with the classic server model.

In 2012, another cloud-related breach took place at the Institute of Electrical and Electronics Engineers (IEEE). The breach was discovered by an independent security researcher who was searching for some literature on IEEE File Transfer Protocol (FTP) servers [15]. The researcher found a cache of 100,000 usernames and passwords in plaintext just sitting there waiting to be grabbed. The credentials included those of members working in Google, Apple, NASA, Standford University, among others. In addition to login credentials, the researcher was able to access more than 100 GB of web server log data containing detailed information on 350 million-plus HTTP requests made by IEEE members over one month. The FTP server this researcher was surfing was a public one. The researcher said that these files were easily accessible on the public servers for over a month. An institution as large and known as IEEE should not have fallen in these naive security errors.

According to the cloud security report, issued by Alert Logic, attacks on cloud computing became almost equal in number to attacks on classic computer systems in 2014 [16]. The report says that brute-force attacks have increase 30 % of all cloud attacks to 44 %. A brute-force attack is an attack that involves large number of trials of credentials to access a certain resource. At the same time, malware attacks on clouds have climbed from 5 % to 11 %.

The *venom* vulnerability can be identified as vulnerability in the code of the virtual floppy that can be exploited to access sensitive and personal data stored on the cloud. Security researchers said that systems run be Microsoft Hyper-V, VMware, and Bochs were not affected by the vulnerability.

Although most organizations affected by this vulnerability said that this vulnerability was never used by any attacker, this vulnerability sends a clear message that cloud security is not perfect. Actually, it is far from perfect. Just like any other component in the field of information security [17].

In 2015, a security services company named Elastica revealed that SalesForce.com servers were vulnerable to a Cross-Site Scripting (XSS) attack. This vulnerability, although it was patched two days before the announcement of its existence, would enable the attacker to run JavaScript to steal the cookies that contain session credentials and hijack the session. The vulnerability is also said to enable the attacker to force SalesForce.com client to phishing websites that can enable the attacker to get credential information through social engineering. The attacker would also be able to force the client to download and run malicious code from the infected application [18].

Later in 2015, a vulnerability was discovered in Amazon cloud storage platform by a group of scientists [19]. The study revealed that a sophisticated CPU cache attack against an Amazon EC2 instance could have given a hacker complete access to a 2048-bit RSA key used in a separate instance hosted at the same physical server. The attacks starts by co-location identification and verification. Then, the attacker would perform a sort of cache attack to detect keys used in RSA encryption. Luckily, this implementation vulnerability was detected on in Libgcrypt RSA implementation libraries.

Another vulnerability, called DROWN, was recently discovered in 2016. This vulnerability was discovered in OpenSSL by a group of 15 scientists [20]. OpenSSL is an open-source implementation of Secure Socket Layer (SSL) security protocol. According to the report, attacker could break HTTPS traffic by leveraging an older attack method from 1998 against SSLv2, even if the server's traffic was protected with newer and more secure Transport Layer Security (TLS) certificates. The report says that around one-third of all websites using HTTPS. When the study was first published in March 1, 2016, Skyhigh Networks, a cloud security company, explains that, during its scans, it detected 653 cloud service providers susceptible to DROWN attacks. Seven days later, 620 out of the 653 cloud services were still unpatched. This shows an example of the lack of timely response by some cloud service providers operating in the market.

References

1. R. Shirey, Rfc 2828: Internet security glossary, in *The Internet Society* (2000), p. 13
2. W. Stallings, *Cryptography and Network Security, 4/E* (Pearson Education, Upper Saddle River, 2006)

3. J. Idziorek, M. Tannian, D. Jacobson, Attribution of fraudulent resource consumption in the cloud, in *Proceedings of the IEEE 5th International Conference on Cloud Computing (CLOUD)*, 2012, pp. 99–106

4. M.M. Alani, Manet security: a survey, in *Proceedings of the IEEE International Conference on Control System, Computing and Engineering (ICCSCE)*, 2014, pp. 559–564

5. R.V. Deshmukh, K.K. Devadkar, Understanding ddos attack & its effect in cloud environment. Procedia Comput. Sci. **49**, 202–210 (2015)

6. M.M. Alani, *Guide to OSI and TCP/IP models* (Springer, Berlin, 2014)

7. J. Graham-Cumming, Understanding and mitigating ntp-based ddos attacks, vol. 9 (Cloudflare Inc, California, 2014)

8. M. Prince, Technical details behind a 400gbps ntp amplification ddos attack, vol. 13 (Cloudflare Inc, California, 2014)

9. N. Gruschka, M. Jensen, Attack surfaces: a taxonomy for attacks on cloud services, in *Proceedings of the IEEE 3rd International Conference on Cloud Computing*, 2010, pp. 276–279

10. Tripadvisor: E-mail addresses stolen in data breach, http://www.cnet.com/news/tripadvisor-e-mail-addresses-stolen-in-data-breach/. Accessed 27 March 2016

11. 6 worst data breaches of 2011, http://www.darkreading.com/attacks-and-breaches/6-worst-data-breaches-of-2011/d/d-id/1102001? Accessed 29 March 2016

12. The sony hack what happened, how did it happen.what did we learn? http://blogs.umb.edu/itnews/2015/01/06/the-sony-hack/. Accessed 29 March 2016

13. Nasdaq server breach: 3 expected findings, http://www.darkreading.com/attacks-and-breaches/nasdaq-server-breach-3-expected-findings/d/d-id/1100934? Accessed 29 March 2016

14. J. Hong, The state of phishing attacks. Commun. ACM **55**(1), 74–81 (2012)

15. Data breach at ieee.org: 100k plaintext passwords, http://ieeelog.dragusin.ro/init/default/log. Accessed 29 March 2016

16. A. Logic, Cloud security report-spring 2014, 2014

17. J.-M. Brook, R. Brooks, A decade of lessons learned: Transforming the enterprise for todays cloud architecture, in *Proceedings of the ICCSM2015 3rd International Conference on Cloud Security and Management: ICCSM2015*, Academic Conferences and publishing limited, 2015, p. 16

18. Salesforce accounts susceptible to hijacking using xss flaw, https://www.elastica.net/salesforce-accounts-susceptible-to-hijacking-using-xss-flaw. Accessed 21 March 2016

19. M.S. Inci, B. Gulmezoglu, G. Irazoqui, T. Eisenbarth, B. Sunar, Seriously, get off my cloud! cross-vm rsa key recovery in a public cloud (Technical report, IACR Cryptology ePrint Archive, 2015)

20. N. Aviram, S. Schinzel, J. Somorovsky, N. Heninger, M. Dankel, J. Steube, L. Valenta, D. Adrian, J.A. Halderman, V. Dukhovni et al., Drown: Breaking tls using sslv2

Chapter 3
Security Threats in Cloud Computing

Abstract This chapter discusses the most common threats in cloud computing. It starts with discussing data breaches and data loss. It also discusses the dangers of account and service hijacking in addition to the use of insecure APIs. The chapter also explains different threats to availability in the cloud and the dangers of malicious insiders. The chapter ends with the explanation of insufficient due diligence along with a few other minor threats.

Keywords Cloud computing · IaaS · PaaS · SaaS · Cloud security · Cloud threats

3.1 Introduction

In Chap. 2, we have identified a threat as a potential for violation of security, which exists when there is a circumstance, capability, action, or event that could breach security and cause harm [1]. In addition to the regular threats to network security, the unique nature of cloud computing creates a different type of threats that are available only in a cloud environment. For example, attacks on cloud components such as hypervisors are not available in the classic network security terminology. In their "The Notorious Nine" report, Cloud Security Alliance (CSA) has identified nine threats that represent most important threats to cloud computing security in the year 2013 [2]. In the coming sections, these threats will be discussed based in order of importance as mentioned in [2].

3.2 Data Breaches

Every security specialist's nightmare starts with a scenario that leads to having the organization's sensitive data falling in the hands of competitors. Even one personal level, the worst that can happen to you is to have your private data publicly available for prying eyes. If your organization provides a cloud-based service to users and part

© The Author(s) 2016
M.M. Alani, *Elements of Cloud Computing Security*,
SpringerBriefs in Computer Science, DOI 10.1007/978-3-319-41411-9_3

of your users' data is leaked, you can say that there is a very high probability that your organization will be out of business soon.

In the scenario of a poorly designed multitenant cloud service, a flaw in one client application could allow an attacker to access the data of that client and all other clients hosted on the same physical machine [3].

In 2012, researchers introduced a side-channel attack, which we will explain in details in Chap. 4, in [4]. This attack enables one Virtual Machine (VM) hosted on a physical machine in the cloud to extract private cryptographic keys used by another virtual machine hosted on the same physical machine. This attack is just an example of how poor design can cause severe data breaches.

As this threat exists in IaaS, SaaS, and PaaS service model, mitigation of it is not a simple task. The interaction between data breaches and data loss is delicate and the emergency plans need to be crafted carefully. One way of eliminating data breaches is to encrypt all of the client data. This encryption is done using a key. To keep information secure, the key should be with the client only and not stored on the cloud itself. However, if the encryption key is lost, the client would have a complete data loss. Thus, the client would need to have a backup copy of the data, somewhere else, or even off-line backup. The client should keep in mind that having more copies of the data would potentially increase the probability of data breaches.

If we think of a data breach in the size of what happened to Sony in 2011 (as explained in the last section of Chap. 2). The attackers took terabytes of private data, deleted the original copies from Sony computers, and left messages threatening to release the information if Sony did not comply with the attackers demands. After the breach, 32,000 private internal and external e-mails were released in public. Passwords and personal information of actors, managers, and Sony staff were publicly available. The cost of this data breach is still growing as you read this book.

The simplest idea to mitigate this threat is encryption. However, the applicability of encryption is not that simple when it comes to the cloud. Many questions will arise when we talk about encryption: Should the encryption happen at the client side or cloud side? If at the cloud side, should the encryption keys be stored at the service provider side or the client side? How can we safely transfer the keys to the cloud? If the encryption happens at the client side, where should decryption happen? What happens if the user loses the encryption keys? and so many other questions that need a proper answer. More details on these challenges can be found in [5, 6].

In [7], a data retrieval scheme using attribute-based encryption was suggested. The scheme is suitable for cloud storage systems with massive amounts of data. It focuses on safeguarding data security and user privacy while retrieving data from cloud storage. The suggested scheme also provides fast search using simple comparisons of searching entities.

A famous scheme was proposed in [8] that focuses on achieving fine-grainedness, scalability, and data confidentiality of access control. In this scheme, access policies based on data attributes were defined and enforced, and, on the other hand, allowing the data owner to delegate most of the computation tasks involved in fine-grained data access control to untrusted cloud servers without disclosing the underlying data contents. The scheme combines techniques of attribute-based encryption (ABE), proxy re-encryption, and lazy re-encryption. However, this scheme was shown later on by [9] that it is vulnerable to an attacked called collusion attack. A *collusion attack* is an attack performed by a revoked user colluding with cloud server to illegally read data.

A technique was introduced in [9] that eliminates collusion attack by dividing the data file into a header and a body to be separately stored to privilege manager group and cloud service provider. If the user is not authorized by privilege manager group, it cannot obtain information regarding the data encryption key within header, so decrypting body is completely impossible.

More detailed discussions of encryption and privacy in the cloud can be found in [5, 10–14].

3.3 Data Loss

Data loss is one of the oldest threats in the information technology field. Reasons behind data loss can vary depending one each network's design. However, we can sum up the main causes of data loss in the following, nonexclusive, list:

1. Malicious attacks.
2. Natural catastrophes such as earthquakes, floods, and fires.
3. Accidental erasure or loss by the cloud client organizations' staff.
4. Accidental erasure or loss by the cloud service provider.

The list shows that the burden of protection from data loss does not fall onto the shoulders of the cloud service provider alone rather on all parties involved. When the loss is caused by a malicious attack, most clients would point their finger toward the cloud service provider. However, this is not always the case. If you look at the examples of attacks we mentioned in Chap. 2, you will see that most of them happen because of some type of misuse by the client. Attacks such as spear phishing and weak passwords are mainly caused by the client rather than the service provider. At the end, we cannot come up with a general rule of "whose fault is it?" when a malicious attack happens. Natural catastrophes are uncontrollable such that the client and the service provider do not have the ability to control it. On the other hand, clients and service providers can reduce the impact of these catastrophes by implementing mitigation techniques that we will discuss before the end of this section.

Accidental erasure or loss by the client's staff can happen in multiple ways. An example of this case is the one mentioned in the previous section; if the client encrypts the data before uploading to the cloud and loses the encryption key, data would be lost.

Client's data can also be erased or lost by the cloud service provider. This erasure can happen deliberately or accidentally. Either way, many organizations dislike the cloud because of this fact. Giving a service provider the control over your data storage is not something that many organizations feel comfortable doing. This is mainly the reason why many organizations create private clouds. In many countries, the organizations are required to keep complete audit logs of their work. If these logs were stored on the cloud and lost, this can jeopardize the existence of the organization and cause many legal issues.

Data loss is considered a threat to the IaaS, SaaS, and PaaS models. Mitigation of this threat can be done through backups. Regular (daily or even hourly) off-line backups can be used to restore data with minimum loss. For services that have zero tolerance for data loss, online backups with a different service provider can be a costly, but safe solution.

In [15], a secure cloud backup system was presented. Although the suggested model uses cloud storage as a backup for any system, it is possible to use it as a backup for another cloud-based system. The paper suggests a model where data can be stored on cloud storage with an added security layer that provides encryption of user data. The model also employs version control, which can be useful in backup scenarios. The suggested model was implemented on Amazon S3 cloud and showed good performance statistics.

A patent registered by Google also introduced a novel cloud backup system. The system is an integration of a distributed backup environment and a online backup environment [16]. In that backup system, a device named a super peer device can be designated from a set of peer interconnected storage devices. The super peer can manage backup data distribution in the set of peer devices based upon availability and storage capacity of the peer devices. In addition, the super peer can transfer portions of backup data from the set of peers to an online backup service.

In [17], a mechanism for online data backup for cloud with disaster recovery was introduced. The suggested approach is said to reduce the cost of the backup solution. The suggested mechanism also serves in simplifying migration from one cloud service provider to another. This solution eliminates consumers dependency on the service provider and also eliminates the associated data backup cost.

Using the cloud as a backup is not as simple as we might think. One issue named data deduplication arises. The term *data deduplication* refers to techniques that store only a single copy of redundant data and provide links to that copy instead of storing other actual copies of the data on multiple VMs [18]. Deduplication has been handled by many researchers and you can find more information in [19–23].

3.4 Account or Service Hijacking

Old attacks such as social engineering and exploiting software vulnerabilities are still in action. These attacks can still achieve the intended result for a malicious attacker. Reusing usernames and passwords magnifies the severity of this threat. In the last section of Chap. 2, we have discussed examples of cloud attacks based on social engineering tricks such as spear phishing and have shown its magnitude in attacks like the one on Epsilon, the cloud-based e-mail service provider.

A new scope is added to these attacks in cloud computing. The attacker, after gaining access to the clients credentials, can eavesdrop on the client transactions, return falsified information, manipulate data, and even redirect the users to illegitimate sites. In addition to that the attacker can use the instances of the client as attacking bases to attack other people. Such access can compromise confidentiality, availability, and integrity. In 2009, Amazon had a large number of their cloud systems hijacked and were used to run Zeus botnet nodes [24]. Zeus is a banking trojan and one of its variants was spotted using the Amazon's cloud service as a command and control channel for infected machines. After the target gets tricked into installing the password-logging malware, their machine began reporting to EC2 for new instructions and updates. On their side, Amazon said that the trojan was using a legitimately bought service that had been compromised using some bugs.

According to [25], in 2010 Amazon.com had a cross-site scripting (XSS) bug that allowed attackers to hijack credentials from the site. The bug on Amazon Wireless allowed attackers to steal the session IDs that are used to grant users access to their accounts after they enter their password. It exposed the credentials of customers who clicked on a specific link while logged into the main Amazon.com page.

This threat exists in IaaS, SaaS, and PaaS models of the could system and its mitigation techniques can vary in their importance. The following list shows the most important mitigation techniques:

- The first mitigation technique is to increase the awareness. Increasing the awareness of the organizations employees can be crucial in reducing the dangers of attacks like phishing and other social engineering techniques. In [26], you can find useful details on how to develop a complete Security Educations, Training, and Awareness (SETA) plan for the organization. It also discusses how such plans can reduce risks of information security in short term and long term.
- Keeping all systems up-to-date and always patching an updating operating systems and protection software is also vital.
- Another important aspect of mitigation is to prohibit account credentials sharing between users and services. The use of two-factor authentication such as password and fingerprint, and password and voiceprint can eliminate this threat to a great extent.
- The client must be aware that there is no way to fully proof the system against these types of attacks. Instead, there are many ways to reduce their probability severely and scenarios of handling these breaches after they happen. This needs a proper incident response and disaster recovery plans.

3.5 Insecure Interfaces and APIs

For the client can manage and interact with the cloud services, the cloud service provider needs to provide a set of Application Programming Interfaces (APIs). These APIs are used for provisioning, management, orchestration, and monitoring.

Availability and security of the cloud service is heavily dependent on the security of these APIs.

Securing the system becomes more complex when the organization builds on these APIs to provide value-added services to their clients. This dependence on APIs shifts their architecture into a layered model. This layered model increases risk by increasing the exposure area of the system. In many scenarios, the organization will have to pass their credentials to a third party to enable them to create or use these new APIs.

While this threat exists on IaaS, SaaS, and PaaS models, it is essential that the clients understand the security implications that come with the usage, management, and monitoring of cloud services.

It is also essential to select a cloud service provider that provides authentication and access control, and encryption and activity-monitoring APIs that are designed to protect against accidental as well as malicious attempts to circumvent the policy.

Depending on poorly designed APIs can compromise the confidentiality, integrity, availability, and accountability. Thus, secure and properly designed APIs must be a necessity by the client when selecting the cloud service provider.

In [27], a discussion about the importance of APIs security was presented. The paper also presented a two-stage API access control mechanism using the Role Based Access Control Model (RBAC). The first stage to ensure that only registered users from white-listed domains can access the cloud service and at the same time extract the required input for the second stage.

Another similar effort was made in [28]. Although it was directed toward mobile cloud, the concept can be applied to nonmobile cloud computing. The paper introduces two multifactor web API security strategies and mechanisms that can be used in providing end-to-end secure client–server architecture.

Most cloud APIs rely on an authentication mechanism that uses an API key. The API key is used for authenticating the access to the cloud. In [29], a discussion about the security concerns of managing those API keys is presented. The paper reviews popular client authentication methods that cloud service providers use. The paper also suggests using cloud hardware secure elements for secure key provisioning, storage, and usage. The suggested scheme replaces manual API key handling with end-to-end security between the cloud service provider and the client's secure elements.

3.6   Threats to Availability

Denial of service (DoS) will be mentioned as a threat and as a type of attack, in Chap. 4, as well. As a threat, DoS exists in almost all networking services. In general, DoS is preventing the service from being provided to its intended audience. This can be through preventing website visitors from viewing the website, blocking legitimate user access to a Voice-over-IP (VoIP) server, etc.

In cloud computing, the situation is slightly worse. DoS would not only render the service unavailable, but also cause huge additional financial implications. Since cloud service providers charge their clients based on the amount of resources they consume, the attacker can cause a huge increase in the bill even if the attacker did not succeed in taking the clients system completely down. Another point that makes this threat even more dangerous in cloud computing is that cloud computing clients share the same infrastructure. Hence, a heavy DoS attack on one client can bring down the whole cloud.

This threat exists in IaaS, SaaS, and PaaS models. In terms of mitigating this threat, there is not much that can be done to prevent it. Being at the receiving end of a DoS attack is analogous to being caught in traffic lock, you cannot get to your destination and you can do nothing about it except waiting. The service outage becomes very frustrating to clients and they start reconsidering the reasons why they moved their data to the cloud.

There is no clearly identified cure to this threat. However, service providers tend to use security appliances such as firewalls, intrusion detection, and intrusion prevention systems that can help in reducing the risk and early detection of the attacks. You can find more information about DoS and DDoS attacks on the cloud in [30].

Detailed discussion of mitigation techniques will be left to Chap. 4, when we discuss DoS as an attack.

3.7 Malicious Insiders

According to [31], 62 % of security professionals saw increase in insider attacks. In the same survey, 59 % of security professionals believe that privileged users such as managers with access to secure data are most risky. Another part of the statistics shows that 62 % of security professional believes that insider attacks are very difficult to detect.

In cloud computing, a malicious insider, despite of the low probability of occurrence in comparison with external attackers, can have a very high magnitude of impact. In [32], it is considered one of the highest possible risks on a cloud computing service. The reason behind that is that cloud architectures necessitate certain roles which are considered of the highest possible risk. An example of these roles is CP system administrators and auditors and managed security service providers dealing with intrusion detection reports and incident response.

Organizations that depend solely on the service provider in security are at great risk due to malicious insiders.

From IaaS to PaaS and SaaS models, the malicious insider can have increasing access levels to more critical data [2].

Encrypting the client data will not completely mitigate this threat. If the encryption keys are not stored with the client and are only available at data usage time, the system is still vulnerable to malicious insider attack. Thus, it is advisable that all client data are encrypted and the keys should be kept with the client.

In [33], a detailed review of the existing trust management research in cloud environments was introduced. The paper also provided a detailed assessment of the research on trust management. This can be useful in the avoidance and detection of insider attacks.

A novel method of detecting malicious insiders and malicious administrators was proposed in [34]. This paper discusses the threats to client data privacy and integrity posed by a malicious cloud administrator. The proposed method is based on protecting privacy and integrity of cloud users workloads against attacks by system administrators during operation and maintenance. This is done by managing the privileges of administrators during operation and maintenance while re-establishing the security of a compute node once administration is completed. The paper also explains how the existing cloud architecture needs to be extended to accommodate the suggested method.

3.8   Abuse of Cloud Service

For most organizations, the main reason behind cloud computing adoption is to facilitate low-cost high-resource solutions. These low-cost solutions can be very beneficial to small companies that require high computing resources for a short period of time. On the other hand, these services can be used by malicious attackers. The access to these huge computing resources can be abused and these resources can be directed toward attacking other systems.

The imminence of this threat has dropped over the past few years due to stricter policies followed by cloud service providers. This threat applies to IaaS and PaaS models.

The only possible way to mitigate this threat is to select a cloud service provider that has strict policies related to service abuse with a quick response time to violations of these policies. There is nothing technical to be done as far as the client is concerned.

In the past few years, there have been many examples of service abuse. As we have discussed earlier in Sect. 4, in 2010 a malicious attacker hijacked cloud services and used them to deploy Zeus botnets [24].

In [35], a thorough discussion of using cloud-based servers to distribute malware was introduced. The paper proposed a technique to detect whether an exploit server is part of a larger organization. The proposed method collects information on how servers are configured and what malware they distribute, and groups servers with similar configurations. The paper states that 60 % of exploit servers was hosted by specialized cloud hosting services. The paper also shows the difficulty of taking down an exploit server by following-up the processes of abuse reporting for exploit servers. The study have shown that after the abuse report, one average, exploit servers live for 4.3 days.

The huge processing power available in the cloud makes it a very tempting tool for attackers. The anonymity provided by IaaS and PaaS service models also unveil critical exploitation possibilities. This anonymity can lead to abuse of the provided infrastructure in conducting DDoS attacks, controlling an army of botnets, hosting malicious data, unlawful distribution of copyrighted data and, last but not least, sending spam e-mails.

3.9 Insufficient Due Diligence

Cloud computing has become the big thing that every organization would like to use. Some companies jump into using cloud computing before being completely prepared. Some preparations need to be made like having a mature understanding of the cloud models, operation, and governance, and understanding why the cloud is a more suitable solution for the organization.

The quick adoption of cloud computing can be a realistic goal for organizations that have the resources required to implement cloud computing properly. Organizations that does not fully comprehend the requirements of proper implementation of cloud computing will have many issues with operational responsibility, incident response, and many other aspects [2].

Organizations with weak understanding of cloud computing can have contractual issues over obligations on liability, response, or transparency. This is caused by mismatch of expectations between the client and the cloud service provider. Security issues might arise by pushing applications that are dependent on internal network-level security controls to the cloud.

Organizations might also face unknown operational and architectural issues when they use designers and architects that are unfamiliar with cloud technologies for their applications. Operational issues such as accounts management and user rights management can hinder the proper operation of the organization's system on the cloud [36].

In [37], a short list of architectural issues that needs to be considered by any organization was introduced, as follows:

- How and who will measure the delivery of services?
- How to develop an agreed method of monitoring performance?
- What will happen if the provider unable or fails to deliver the services as contract?
- What will be the mechanism to change SLA over time?
- What will be the compensation mechanism if service provider violates any elements of the SLA?

If the organization does not understand the full scope of the transfer from the classic network service architecture to the cloud-based service architecture, it will not be able to succeed in using the cloud and might prefer a quick fallback to the classical model.

A worse case is when an unprepared organization takes the decision to create their own private cloud. While some organizations make a conscious decision to create their own cloud without considering the requirements, other organizations are forced by law to keep their data in the house. Government organizations, for example, in many countries are forced to keep their sensitive and private data inside their premises.

It feels much safer to keep your data in your organization. However, this feeling might be false security if your organization is not technically capable of handling a privately owned cloud. In [38], the main disadvantages of private clouds were summarized in the following two points:

1. Cost: The capital expenditure for setting up a private clouds is very high because they require buying hardware and software licenses. In addition to the capital expenditure, operational expenditure is high as well. Operational expenditures include cost of electrical power (primary and backup), hardware and software maintenance, competent system administrators, maintenance personnel, among others.
2. Maintenance: The cloud is all about availability. It is not possible to setup a cloud without providing proper maintenance plan. This includes continuous power availability (through generators, backup generators, and uninterruptible power supplies), server hardware maintenance, server software maintenance, incident response plan, disaster recovery plan, and business continuity plan, etc.

Many aspects need to be studied before making a decision to setup a private cloud. In some countries, such as the United Arab Emirates, the government understands the requirements and creates a single governmental cloud to be shared by different government departments. This gives many benefits to the governmental organization such as cost saving, better security, removing the need for highly qualified maintenance staff, release from the complicated incident response, and disaster recovery plans for the cloud.

This threat applies to IaaS, SaaS, and PaaS models. A reasonable mitigation technique for this threat would be a proper organizational understanding of the cloud computing service models and the duties and capabilities of the organization. Whether the organization chooses to go for public cloud service or private cloud service, the organization must assure the availability of the information technological resources and human resources required for the proper operation of the cloud.

3.10 Shared Technology Vulnerabilities

As discussed earlier in Chap. 1, cloud computing relies on many backend technologies to provide its services. Any vulnerability existing at the backend can lead to full-system exploitation in all clients. There were cases where the underlying architecture (such as CPU caches, GPUs, etc.) does not provide complete isolation properties. This can enable the attacker to use one client VM to exploit other clients.

When an integral part is compromised, such as the hypervisor, it exposes not only the compromised client, but also the entire environment. Although this threat is considered dangerous because it can affect a complete cloud all at once, its severity has dropped over the past few years. This drop is due to more accurate configuration and isolation by the hardware manufacturers and the cloud service providers.

This threat exists in IaaS, SaaS, and PaaS models. The mitigation of this threat is to be done by the cloud service provider. Keeping systems updated and giving high attention to configuration can reduce the probability of exploiting such vulnerability at the backend.

A very thorough study of the open source code of two very popular hypervisors, Xen and KVM, was conducted in [39]. The paper suggested a characterization of hypervisor vulnerabilities in three dimensions: the trigger source (i.e., where the attacker is located), the attack vector (i.e., the hypervisor functionality that enables the security breach), and the attack target (i.e., the runtime domain that is compromised). This characterization can help in understanding potential paths different attacks can take, which vulnerabilities enable them, and where the defenses should be focused.

In addition to hypervisor threats, other shared technology attacks are possible. In [40], a description of three misuse patterns was introduced. The paper focused on presenting these misuse attacks from the eye of the attacker. The three misuse patterns discussed in the paper were resource usage monitoring inference, malicious virtual machine creation, and malicious virtual machine migration process.

It was stated in [5] that adoption problems arising in cloud computing are essentially old problems in new settings. The paper also states that virtual machine attacks and web service vulnerabilities existed long before cloud computing became fashionable.

As long as different virtual machines in the cloud are sharing memory spaces, hard disk spaces, cache memory, and other hardware components, there will always be room for the threats we have mentioned earlier. It is expected that the future developments in hardware will drive toward more isolation between hosted virtual machines. This increased isolation will be very beneficial in terms of security.

3.11 Other Threats

There are other threats to cloud computing systems that have varying severity. The following list provides some of the other threats that are thought of as less severe and they were not mentioned in the Notorious Nine report in [2]:

- **Lock-in** [41]
  Currently, there are no clear rules that govern the portability of data and services. If a client wishes discontinue service at one cloud service provider and to change provider, many issues may arise. This is one threat that makes many organizations think twice before choosing their cloud service provider to make sure that they will not need to switch to another service provider any time soon.
- **Insecure or Incomplete Data Deletion** [41]
  We know that in a regular operating system, deleted data do not get wiped from the disk immediately. The data rather sit there and wait to be overwritten. In a cloud service, data are stored on someone else's disk. Thus, when a request to delete a

cloud resource is made, as with most operating systems, this may not result in true wiping of the data. This can cause problems if a malicious attacker gets a legitimate virtual machine over the old, and supposedly deleted, target virtual machine.

- **Loss of Governance** [41]
  Service Level Agreement (SLA) is a very important document that governs the relationship between the client and the cloud service provider. The SLA usually explains the rights and obligations of each side. Many issues can arise because of the SLA. There are some cases in which the SLA does not cover all security aspects such that the client is unclear about which measures need to be taken by the client and which by the cloud service provider. Some other issues arise because the client does not read the SLA carefully and depends solely on the service provider.

- **Acquisition of the cloud provider** [41]
  Over the past few years, many information technology service providers were bought by other, usually larger, organizations. Some other companies were merged together. In this scenario, there is a very good likelihood of a strategic shift in the service provider strategy and may put nonbinding agreements at risk of cancelation or change.

- **Threats to Trust** [42] As trust is not a new concept in computer science, in the context of cloud computing it focuses on convincing observers that a system (model, design, or implementation) was correct and secure [43]. The concept of trust, adjusted to the case of two parties involved in a transaction, can be described as follows: An entity A is considered to trust another entity B when entity A believes that entity B will behave exactly as expected and required [42]. Afterward, we can consider the entity trustworthy, if the parties involved in transactions with that entity rely on its credibility.
  In the cloud computing environment, trust depends on the selected deployment model, as governance of data and applications is outsourced and delegated out of the owners strict control. In the case of public or community clouds, control is delegated to the organization owning the infrastructure. When deploying on a public cloud, control is mitigated to the infrastructure owner to enforce a sufficient security policy that guarantees that appropriate security activities are being performed to ensure that risk is reduced. Deployment in public clouds and community clouds introduces a number of risks and threats, as essential security is related to trusting the processes and computing base implemented by the cloud owner rather than the data owner.

- **Difficulty in Forensics Analysis After Security Breaches** [44] In information security, whenever security breach, policy violation, or other security incident occur, a forensics investigation is necessary. Forensics investigation helps in detecting reasons behind the incident and how to prevent it from happening in the future. Almost all of the current forensics investigation tools and concepts are designed for off-line investigation. Also, it is always assumed that the storage media under investigation is under full control of the investigator. However, in the cloud environment forensic investigation can be quite challenging. In the cloud, evidence is likely to be ephemeral and stored on media beyond the immediate control of an investigator.

References

1. R. Shirey, Rfc 2828: Internet security glossary, in *The Internet Society*, p. 13 (2000)
2. T.T.W. Group et al., The notorious nine: cloud computing top threats in 2013, in *Cloud Security Alliance* (2013)
3. F. Chong, G. Carraro, R. Wolter, Multi-tenant data architecture, in *MSDN Library, Microsoft Corporation*, pp. 14–30 (2006)
4. Y. Zhang, A. Juels, A. Oprea, M.K. Reiter, Homealone: co-residency detection in the cloud via side-channel analysis, in *2011 IEEE Symposium on Security and Privacy (SP)* (IEEE, 2011), pp. 313–328
5. R. Chow, P. Golle, M. Jakobsson, E. Shi, J. Staddon, R. Masuoka, J. Molina, Controlling data in the cloud: outsourcing computation without outsourcing control, in *Proceedings of the 2009 ACM Workshop on Cloud Computing Security* (ACM, 2009), pp. 85–90
6. H. Takabi, J.B. Joshi, G.-J. Ahn, Security and privacy challenges in cloud computing environments. IEEE Secur. Priv. **6**, 24–31 (2010)
7. D. Koo, J. Hur, H. Yoon, Secure and efficient data retrieval over encrypted data using attribute-based encryption in cloud storage. Comput. Electr. Eng. **39**(1), 34–46 (2013)
8. S. Yu, C. Wang, K. Ren, W. Lou, Achieving secure, scalable, and fine-grained data access control in cloud computing, in *Proceedings of the IEEE Infocom, 2010* (IEEE, 2010), pp. 1–9
9. N. Park, *Secure data access control scheme using type-based re-encryption in cloud environment, in Semantic Methods for Knowledge Management and Communication* (Springer, Berlin, 2011), pp. 319–327
10. C.-I. Fan, S.-Y. Huang, Controllable privacy preserving search based on symmetric predicate encryption in cloud storage. Future Gener. Comput. Syst. **29**(7), 1716–1724 (2013)
11. F. Fatemi Moghaddam, O. Karimi, M.T. Alrashdan, A comparative study of applying real-time encryption in cloud computing environments, in *2013 IEEE 2nd International Conference on Cloud Networking (CloudNet)* (IEEE, 2013), pp. 185–189
12. U. Somani, K. Lakhani, M. Mundra, Implementing digital signature with RSA encryption algorithm to enhance the data security of cloud in cloud computing, in *2010 1st International Conference on Parallel Distributed and Grid Computing (PDGC)* (IEEE, 2010), pp. 211–216
13. M. Li, S. Yu, Y. Zheng, K. Ren, W. Lou, Scalable and secure sharing of personal health records in cloud computing using attribute-based encryption. IEEE Trans. Parallel Distrib. Syst. **24**(1), 131–143 (2013)
14. K. Liang, M.H. Au, J.K. Liu, W. Susilo, D.S. Wong, G. Yang, Y. Yu, A. Yang, A secure and efficient ciphertext-policy attribute-based proxy re-encryption for cloud data sharing. Future Gener. Comput. Syst. **52**, 95–108 (2015)
15. A. Rahumed, H.C. Chen, Y. Tang, P.P. Lee, J. Lui, A secure cloud backup system with assured deletion and version control, in *2011 40th International Conference on Parallel Processing Workshops (ICPPW)* (IEEE, 2011), pp. 160–167
16. J.D. Mehr, E.E. Murphy, N. Virk, L.M. Sosnosky, Hybrid distributed and cloud backup architecture. US Patent 8,935,366, 13 Jan 2015
17. V. Javaraiah, Backup for cloud and disaster recovery for consumers and smbs, in *2011 IEEE 5th International Conference on Advanced Networks and Telecommunication Systems (ANTS)* (IEEE, 2011), pp. 1–3
18. D. Harnik, B. Pinkas, A. Shulman-Peleg, Side channels in cloud services: deduplication in cloud storage. IEEE Secur. Priv. **8**(6), 40–47 (2010)
19. Y. Fu, H. Jian, N. Xiao, L. Tian, F. Liu, Aa-dedupe: an application-aware source deduplication approach for cloud backup services in the personal computing environment, in *2011 IEEE International Conference on Cluster Computing (CLUSTER)* (IEEE, 2011), pp. 112–120
20. Y. Tan, H. Jiang, D. Feng, L. Tian, Z. Yan, Cabdedupe: a causality-based deduplication performance booster for cloud backup services, in *2011 IEEE International Parallel and Distributed Processing Symposium (IPDPS)* (IEEE, 2011), pp. 1266–1277

21. Y. Tan, H. Jiang, D. Feng, L. Tian, Z. Yan, G. Zhou, Sam: a semantic-aware multi-tiered source de-duplication framework for cloud backup, in *2010 39th International Conference on Parallel Processing (ICPP)* (IEEE, 2010), pp. 614–623

22. J. Stanek, A. Sorniotti, E. Androulaki, L. Kencl, *A secure data deduplication scheme for cloud storage, in Financial Cryptography and Data Security* (Springer, Berlin, 2014), pp. 99–118

23. M. Bellare, S. Keelveedhi, T. Ristenpart, *Message-locked encryption and secure deduplication, in Advances in Cryptology-EUROCRYPT* (Springer, Berlin, 2013), pp. 296–312

24. Zeus bot found using Amazons EC2 as C and C server, http://goo.gl/g9PCtQ. Accessed 30 March 2016

25. Amazon purges account hijacking threat from site, http://goo.gl/JJqxtd. Accessed 30 March 2016

26. A. McIlwraith, *Information Security and Employee Behaviour: How to Reduce Risk Through Employee Education, Training and Awareness* (Gower Publishing Ltd, UK, 2006)

27. A. Sirisha, G.G. Kumari, API access control in cloud using the role based access control model. Trendz Inf. Sci. Comput. (TISC) **2010**, 135–137 (2010)

28. L. Tang, L. Ouyang, W.T. Tsai, Multi-factor web api security for securing mobile cloud, in *2015 12th International Conference on Fuzzy Systems and Knowledge Discovery (FSKD)* (2015), pp. 2163–2168

29. H.K. Lu, Keeping your api keys in a safe, in *2014 IEEE 7th International Conference on Cloud Computing (CLOUD)* (2014), pp. 962–965

30. M. Alani, Securing the cloud against distributed denial of service attacks: a review, in *2nd International Conference of Applied Information and Communications Technologies* (Elsevier, 2014)

31. Veriato, Insider threat spotlight report, http://goo.gl/rcGKcQ. Accessed 30 March 2016

32. Y. Zhang, A. Juels, M.K. Reiter, T. Ristenpart, Cross-vm side channels and their use to extract private keys, in *Proceedings of the 2012 ACM Conference on Computer and Communications Security* (ACM, 2012), pp. 305–316

33. T.H. Noor, Q.Z. Sheng, S. Zeadally, J. Yu, Trust management of services in cloud environments: obstacles and solutions. ACM Comput. Surv. (CSUR) **46**(1), 12 (2013)

34. S. Bleikertz, A. Kurmus, Z.A. Nagy, M. Schunter, Secure cloud maintenance: protecting workloads against insider attacks, in *Proceedings of the 7th ACM Symposium on Information, Computer and Communications Security* (ACM, 2012), pp. 83–84

35. A. Nappa, M.Z. Rafique, J. Caballero, *Driving in the cloud: an analysis of drive-by download operations and abuse reporting, in Detection of Intrusions and Malware, and Vulnerability Assessment* (Springer, Berlin, 2013), pp. 1–20

36. S.K. Nair, S. Porwal, T. Dimitrakos, A.J. Ferrer, J. Tordsson, T. Sharif, C. Sheridan, M. Rajarajan, A.U. Khan, Towards secure cloud bursting, brokerage and aggregation, in *2010 IEEE 8th European Conference on Web Services (ECOWS)* (2010), pp. 189–196

37. B.P. Rimal, A. Jukan, D. Katsaros, Y. Goeleven, Architectural requirements for cloud computing systems: an enterprise cloud approach. J. Grid Comput. **9**(1), 3–26 (2011)

38. M. Amini, N. Sadat Safavi, D. Khavidak, S. Mojtaba, A. Abdollahzadegan, Types of cloud computing (public and private) that transform the organization more effectively. Int. J. Eng. Res. Technol. (IJERT) **2**(5), pp. 1263–1269 (2013)

39. D. Perez-Botero, J. Szefer, R.B. Lee, Characterizing hypervisor vulnerabilities in cloud computing servers, in *Proceedings of the 2013 International Workshop on Security in Cloud Computing (Cloud Computing'13)* (ACM, 2013), pp. 3–10

40. K. Hashizume, N. Yoshioka, E.B. Fernandez, *Three misuse patterns for cloud computing, in Security Engineering for Cloud Computing: Approaches and Tools* (Pennsylvania, IGI Global, 2012), pp. 36–53

41. E. Network, I.S. Agency, *Cloud Computing: Benefits, Risks and Recommendations for Information Security* (ENISA, Heraklion, 2009)

42. D. Zissis, D. Lekkas, Addressing cloud computing security issues. Future Gener. Comput. Syst. **28**(3), 583–592 (2012)

43. A. Nagarajan, V. Varadharajan, Dynamic trust enhanced security model for trusted platform based services. Future Gener. Comput. Syst. **27**(5), 564–573 (2011)
44. G. Grispos, T. Storer, W.B. Glisson, Calm before the storm: the challenges of cloud. Emerg. Dig. Forensics Appl. Crime Detect. Prev. Secur. **4**(1), 28–48 (2013)

Chapter 4
Security Attacks in Cloud Computing

Abstract This chapter discusses the most common attacks in cloud computing. It starts with discussing different types of denial of service attacks. It also discusses different attacks on hypervisors. The chapter also explains different attacks on confidentiality of user data in the cloud and resource-freeing attacks. The chapter also explains side-channel attacks. The chapter ends with a simple explanation of other, less significant attacks.

Keywords Cloud computing · IaaS · PaaS · SaaS · Cloud security · Cloud attacks

4.1 Introduction

In Chap. 2, we have identified an attack as an assault on system security that derives from an intelligent threat, i.e., an intelligent act that is a deliberate attempt to evade security services and violate the security policy of a system [1]. Cloud computing, as any other platform, is a target for many attacks. These attacks have different aims starting from reconnaissance, to eavesdropping, and all the way up to complete system failure. Some attackers conduct these attacks as a political statement. However, the main common factor in all of these attacks is that all of them are for malicious purposes. In the following section, we will discuss the most commonly known attacks and some mitigation techniques.

4.2 Denial of Service Attacks

As discussed earlier in Chap. 3, DoS attacks try to render the service unavailable to its legitimate users. The attack consumes large amounts of system resources such as processing power, memory, and bandwidth. This consumption will leave the service inaccessible to the users or intolerably slow.

Attackers can conduct a DoS on one or more layer of the network. DoS attack can be executed on the physical level to render the whole physical machine

© The Author(s) 2016
M.M. Alani, *Elements of Cloud Computing Security*,
SpringerBriefs in Computer Science, DOI 10.1007/978-3-319-41411-9_4

Fig. 4.1 Classification of
Denial of Service attacks

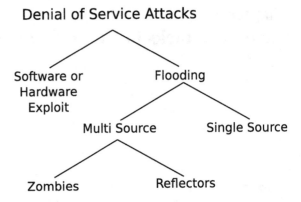

unreachable. The attack can also be conducted on the network layer such that the VM is unreachable. This is done by getting the Network Interface Card (NIC) of the server completely occupied with useless packets in such a way that no more bandwidth is available for legitimate users. A DoS attack can also be launched at the transport layer using the very old, but still effective, SYN Flood technique. In a SYN flood attack, the attacker sends a flood of TCP SYN requests that get the server busy without actually completing the three-way handshake procedure used in the setup of TCP sessions. DoS attacks can also be launched at the application level by sending fake requests to the application layer protocol to consume the server memory and processing power. Sending a flood of fake SMTP requests to an e-mail server is a clear example.

In [2], DoS attacks were classified according to their operating mechanisms. As shown in Fig. 4.1, DoS attacks can be classified based on the amount of packets used in the attacks and later based on the number of attack sources participating in the attack.

DoS attacks that depend on a software or hardware exploit usually come from a single attacker. This attacker is capable, relying on the unnoticed exploit, of taking down the system single-handedly. This type of attack allows a malicious attacker to bring down an application using very small attack payload, sometimes as small as 100 bytes. Several defense mechanisms can be employed like continuous patching and updating the software and firmware, penetration testing, and using firewalls and intrusion detection systems.

Flooding is the most common method of DoS attacks. The idea of flooding is simple; overwhelming the server(s) with a very large amount of requests that the server(s) cannot handle. As we have discussed in Chap. 3, when the flooding requests are coming from a single source, it is easy to track and block. Many security appliances are currently capable of easily detecting simple DoS attacks that come from a single attacking node. Thus, DoS attacks have evolved into a more complicated attack called Distributed DoS (DDoS). In DDoS, the DoS attack is performed from multiple sources around the Internet such that it would be harder to trace and block the attacker. More information about DDoS in cloud computing can be found in [3].

Although DDoS take major attention in the media, it is not the only threatening type of DoS attacks.

The multiple sources used in flooding attacks can be categorized into two types; zombies and reflectors. A *zombie* is a compromised host under control by the attacker. Usually, the attacker implants malicious code into the zombie and gives orders to attack the target or the attack is timed. A *reflector* is a server designed to provide a legitimate service and gets abuse to participate in performing an orchestrated DDoS attack. In the case of employing reflectors, the attacker spoofs the source IP address in the client request and gives the IP address of the target. This way, the server will consider this a legitimate request and sends a reply to the target. The idea is to send and overwhelm amount of replies from multiple servers to the target at the same time. An example was discussed earlier in Chap. 2.

Specific mitigation techniques depend on the type of the DoS attack. In [4], a method that depends on covariance matrix was used to detect DoS attacks. This method was proven to be highly effective in detecting DoS attacks that are based on flooding. The proposed method consists of three phases; the first phase is to model the normal traffic pattern for baseline profiling, the second phase is the intrusion detection processes, and finally the prevention phase.

A new DoS attack along with its countermeasure was introduced in [5]. In this attack, the attacker gathers information about aggregated links in the data center. These uplinks can be considered as bottlenecks in the network. This attack operates on the application level to detect a network bottleneck in one of the links and focus on flooding this link from multiple hosts located on different physical machines. These hosts are then used to send bogus traffic to flood the aggregated uplink and render the network unusable. The suggested mitigation technique is a user-side solution, which does not require any cloud service provider cooperation. Thus, even in a data center that does not have any countermeasures the proposed technique can be employed.

One research direction has employed game theory defense mechanisms in defending the cloud infrastructure against a special type of DoS attacks called coresident DoS attack. In coresident DoS attack, the attacker rents a VM inside the public cloud and conducts the DoS from the rented VM onto another VM within the same physical node. The attacker uses simple tools (such as nmap and hping) to deduce the exact location of the VM in the cloud and conduct a DoS attack on the bottleneck network channel shared among the VMs. In [6], a detection method that is based on game theory defense mechanisms was introduced. The paper evaluates the behavior of a shared network channel using Click modular router on DETER test bed. The paper also illustrates that game theoretic concepts can be used to model this attack as a two-player game and recommend strategies for defending against such attacks.

A model to prevent flooding attacks was introduced in [7]. The paper proposed a model for the prevention of DoS attacks for clouds called FAPA (Flooding Attack Prevention Architecture). This paper's goal was to design a model that allows a dynamic response that can adapt to prevent any type of flooding attack. This model can provide the foundation of further study in the topic of DoS flooding attack prevention.

Another research direction based on Software-Defined Network (SDN) was introduced on [8]. The paper claims that SDN technology can actually help enterprises to defend against DDoS attacks if the defense architecture is designed properly. The paper proposed a DDoS attack mitigation architecture that integrates a highly programmable network monitoring to enable attack detection and a flexible control structure to allow fast and specific attack reaction. To cope with the new architecture, the paper proposed a graphic model-based attack detection system that can deal with the dataset shift problem. The proposed architecture can serve in defending many other attack, not just DDoS.

More DoS and DDoS detection and prevention methods can be found in [9–13].

4.3 Attacks on Hypervisor

As explained earlier, a hypervisor is the abstraction layer software that sits between the hardware and the VMs that comprise the cloud. Although not many attacks were conducted on hypervisors, any compromise in the hypervisor security can bring the whole cloud down.

Hyperjacking was identified in [14] as the attackers attempt to craft and run a very thin hypervisor that takes complete control of the underlying operating system. Once the attacker gains full control of the operating system, the whole cloud is compromised. The attacker will be able to eavesdrop, manipulate client data, disrupt, or even shut down the complete cloud service. Although the probability of this attack succeeding is very low, it is still a source of concern.

In [15], a novel virtualization security solution which aims to provide comprehensive protection of the virtualization environment was proposed. The proposed solution has the strength of protected in-VM monitoring and at the same time leverages the Linux Security Module (LSM) using SELinux. The suggested model is said to protect guest VMs as well as hypervisors from attacks.

A hypervisor vulnerability was previously reported in [16]. This vulnerability was found in many commercial VM and cloud computing products. The vulnerability enables privilege escalation from guest account privileges to host account privileges. The vulnerability was defined as:

"Some 64-bit operating systems and virtualization software running on Intel CPU hardware are vulnerable to a local privilege escalation attack. The vulnerability may be exploited for local privilege escalation or a guest-to-host virtual machine escape. Intel claims that this vulnerability is a software implementation issue, as their processors are functioning as per their documented specifications. However, software that fails to take the Intel-specific SYSRET behavior into account may be vulnerable."

In [17], a turnaround was suggested. The paper suggested the elimination of the hypervisor attack surface by enabling the guest VMs to run natively on the underlying hardware while maintaining the capability of running multiple VMs at the same time. The *NoHype* system proposed was based on 4 main concepts:

1. Preallocation of processor cores and memory resources.
2. Use of virtualized I/O devices.
3. Minor modifications to the guest OS to perform all system discovery during bootup.
4. Avoiding indirection by bringing the guest virtual machine in more direct contact with the underlying hardware.

Another mitigation technique was suggested in [18] through employing a hierarchical secure virtualization model. The paper suggested a hierarchical model that employs a technique of threat quarantine and conquers in addition to complete control on virtualization. The Hierarchical Secure Virtualization Model (HSVM) introduced in the paper focuses on better isolation layering and needs to run under the virtualization level and eventually moves up to the guest OS. The suggested model is said to be operable in IaaS, PaaS, and SaaS cloud service models.

In [19], a hardware protection scheme for VMs was suggested. This hardware protection scheme would protect the VMs from a compromised hypervisor while keeping the flexibility to manage the cloud environment required by the hypervisor. The proposed method applies to multicore multiprocessor systems working in IaaS model only.

More details on hypervisor vulnerabilities can be found in [20].

4.4 Resource Freeing Attacks

When multiple VMs share the same physical node in a cloud, the performance of any given VM will degrade if another VM is overusing the resources. Research conducted in [21] has shown that the performance of a cache-sensitive benchmark can degrade by more than 80 % because of interference from another VM.

The goal of the Resource Freeing Attack (RFA)was to modify the workload of a victim VM in a way that frees up resources for the attackers VM, given that they are sharing the same host machine. The paper explores in-depth a particular example of an RFA. Counterintuitively, by adding load to a coresident victim, the attack speeds up a class of cache-bound workloads. The paper showed that this attack can improve performance of synthetic benchmarks by up to 60 % over not running the attack. While in more crowded cloud environment such as Amazons EC2, the attack improved the performance of the attacker's VM by 13 %.

4.5 Side-Channel Attacks

In a *side-channel attack*, the attacker gains information about the cryptographic technique currently in use through detailed analysis of physical characteristics of the cryptosystem's implementation. The attacker uses information about the timing, power consumption, electromagnetic leaks, etc., to exploit the system. This collected information can be employed in finding sensitive information about the cryptographic system in use. For example, information about power consumption can result in knowing the key used in encryption.

These attacks, although being relatively easy to implementation, can result in dangerous exploitations that can render the whole cryptosystem worthless. More information about side-channel attacks can be found in [22].

In cloud computing, side-channels attacks are conducted through gaining access to the physical node hosting the target VM. This access can be available through creating a VM in the same physical node that is hosting the target VM. This is particularly possible in public clouds. The attacker can keep creating VMs in the cloud until one VM is created in the same physical node of the target VM. Afterward, the attacker can start collecting information necessary to conduct the attack. A method to do this was introduced in [23].

Many researchers focused in their side-channel attacks research on cache memory. In [24], the research focused on threats on the L2 covert channels and how these threats can be exploited or countered. The paper demonstrated the limits of these channels by providing a quantification of the channel bit rates and an assessment of its ability to do harm. While the paper demonstrated a covert channel with considerably higher bit rate than previously reported, the paper states that even at such improved rates, the harm of data extraction from these channels is still limited to the sharing of small, if important, secrets such as private keys.// Research was also done on attacking AES encryption in a virtualized environment. In this attack, the attacker was able to extract sensitive keying material from an isolated trusted execution domain using Bernstein's correlation [25]. The paper showed that the isolation characteristic of system virtualization can be bypassed by the use of a cache-timing attack. The paper stated that an attacker who gained access to the untrusted domain can extract the key of an AES-based authentication protocol used for a financial transaction.

Research on timing channels and their determination in cloud computing was conducted in [26]. This research proposed using provider-enforced deterministic execution as a replacement of resource partitioning to eliminate timing channels within a shared cloud domain.

Many researchers tackled countering side-channel attacks. Papers such as [27] discussed mitigating side-channel attacks in different environments. This paper proposed a general mitigation strategy that focuses on the infrastructure used to measure side-channel leaks rather than the source of leaks. The proposed technique can be applied to all known and unknown microarchitectural side-channel leaks.

More cloud computing-oriented research on the mitigation of side-channel attacks was introduced in [28]. This paper proposed an approach that leverages dynamic cache coloring. The proposed dynamic cache coloring is by notifying the VM management software to swap the process data to a safe and isolated cache line whenever the application is handling security-sensitive data. The performance degradation caused by this method is less when compared to other techniques to mitigate cache side-channel attacks.

A similar method was later introduced in [29]. STEALTHMEM that was introduced in this paper is a system-level protection mechanism designed to counter cache side-channel attacks in a cloud computing environment. The suggested system contains a set of locked cache lines for each core. These cache lines are never evicted from the cache and the system efficiently multiplexes them so that each VM would be capable of loading its own sensitive data into the locked cache. In this way, any VM on the physical node can hide memory access patterns of confidential data from other VMs.

In [30], a method for averting side-channel attack was introduced. The paper proposed using a combination of virtual firewall appliance and random encryption and decryption to achieve confusion and diffusion and provide security to client's data.

More cloud-based side-channel attacks mitigation techniques were introduced in [31–35].

4.6 Attacks on Confidentiality

It is a major concern for all cloud computing clients to secure their data. The confidentiality intended by clients is not only to protect their data from public attacks, but also to protect their data from their cloud service provider. Clients would not accept that their service provider is capable of accessing their private data whenever they want. Thus, clients use encryption.

Confidentiality has always been a target for security attacks since the start of computers. In cloud computing, confidentiality is not only about client data confidentiality. Confidentiality is required in the cloud infrastructure as well. Exploiting private cloud information such as encryption keys, VM locations, or operating system information can lead to more dangerous attacks.

A nontechnical attack can be conducted through social engineering. In a such attack, that attacker can get private information such as encryption keys, passwords, and usernames by tricking privileged users into giving access to their accounts. There is no single specific form this attack takes. It can be mostly done by the attacker impersonating the identity of an IT-support technician, system administrator, or any other person that can have access to private information. The best way to counter this attack through educating users about the nature and shape of these attacks and sometimes additional institutional policies can reduce the probability of such attacks occurrence.

Many other attacks on confidentiality can be orchestrated through side-channel attacks. In [36], an attack was conducted by mapping the internal cloud infrastructure, identifying where a particular VM is likely to reside, and then initiating VMs until one of them is coresident with the target VM in the same physical machine. Afterward, the attacker used this coresident placement to mount cross-virtual machine side-channel attacks to extract information from the target VM that lies within the same physical machine. Amazon EC2 public cloud service was used for case study to conduct the attack. The first part of the procedure is similar to the approach used in [6] to conduct DoS attack.

Side-channel attacks were also employed in [37] but this time it was used to extract private keys used in client data encryption. This attack was the first of its kinds that was demonstrated on a symmetric multiprocessing system with Xen virtualization. The attacker was able to retrieve encryption keys of ElGamal [38, 39] encryption algorithm use in the target VM. In [40], a different approach for securing data confidentiality was introduced. The proposed approach uses offensive decoy technology. The paper suggests monitoring data access patterns. When unauthorized access is suspected and then verified using challenge questions, a disinformation attack is launched by returning large amounts of decoy information to the attacker.

4.7   Other Attacks

In addition to the attacks described earlier, other attacks exist. More information about other attacks can be found in [41–46].

References

1. R. Shirey, Rfc 2828: Internet security glossary, in *The Internet Society* (2000), p. 13
2. A. Hussain, J. Heidemann, C. Papadopoulos, A framework for classifying denial of service attacks, in *Proceedings of the 2003 Conference on Applications, Technologies, Architectures, and Protocols for Computer Communications* (ACM, New York, 2003), pp. 99–110
3. N. Kumar, S. Sharma, Study of intrusion detection system for DDoS attacks in cloud computing, in *2013 Tenth International Conference on Wireless and Optical Communications Networks (WOCN)* (IEEE, New York, 2013), pp. 1–5
4. M.N. Ismail, A. Aborujilah, S. Musa, A. Shahzad, Detecting flooding based dos attack in cloud computing environment using covariance matrix approach, in *Proceedings of the 7th International Conference on Ubiquitous Information Management and Communication* (ACM, New York, 2013), p. 36
5. H. Liu, A new form of dos attack in a cloud and its avoidance mechanism, in *Proceedings of the 2010 ACM Workshop on Cloud Computing Security Workshop* (ACM, New York, 2010), pp. 65–76
6. H.S. Bedi, S. Shiva, Securing cloud infrastructure against co-resident dos attacks using game theoretic defense mechanisms, in *Proceedings of the International Conference on Advances in Computing, Communications and Informatics* (ACM, New York, 2012), pp. 463–469
7. K. Zunnurhain, Fapa: a model to prevent flooding attacks in clouds, in *Proceedings of the 50th Annual Southeast Regional Conference* (ACM, New York, 2012), pp. 395–396
8. B. Wang, Y. Zheng, W. Lou, Y.T. Hou, DDoS attack protection in the era of cloud computing and software-defined networking. Comput. Netw. **81**, 308–319 (2015)

9. T. Karnwal, S. Thandapanii, A. Gnanasekaran, *A filter tree approach to protect cloud computing against xml DDoS and http DDoS attack, in Intelligent Informatics* (Springer, Heidelberg, 2013), pp. 459–469

10. V. Chouhan, S.K. Peddoju, Hierarchical storage technique for maintaining hop-count to prevent ddos attack in cloud computing, in *Proceedings of International Conference on Advances in Computing* (Springer, Heidelberg, 2013), pp. 511–518

11. S. Gupta, P. Kumar, *Vm profile based optimized network attack pattern detection scheme for DDoS attacks in cloud, in Security in Computing and Communications* (Springer, Heidelberg, 2013), pp. 255–261

12. D. Contractor, D.R. Patel, *Trust management framework for attenuation of application layer DDoS attack in cloud computing, in Trust Management VI* (Springer, Heidelberg, 2012), pp. 201–208

13. S. Yu, *Distributed Denial of Service Attack and Defense* (Springer, Heidelberg, 2014)

14. E. Ray, E. Schultz, Virtualization security, in *Proceedings of the 5th Annual Workshop on Cyber Security and Information Intelligence Research: Cyber Security and Information Intelligence Challenges and Strategies* (ACM, New York, 2009), p. 42

15. T.Y. Win, H. Tianfield, Q. Mair, Virtualization security combining mandatory access control and virtual machine introspection, in *Proceedings of the 2014 IEEE/ACM 7th International Conference on Utility and Cloud Computing* (IEEE Computer Society, New York, 2014), pp. 1004–1009

16. C.V.N. VU, Vulnerability note vu no 649219

17. J. Szefer, E. Keller, R.B. Lee, J. Rexford, Eliminating the hypervisor attack surface for a more secure cloud, in *Proceedings of the 18th ACM Conference on Computer and Communications Security* (ACM, New York, 2011), pp. 401–412

18. S. Manavi, S. Mohammadalian, N.I. Udzir, A. Abdullah, Hierarchical secure virtualization model for cloud, in *2012 International Conference on Cyber Security, Cyber Warfare and Digital Forensic (CyberSec)* (IEEE, New York, 2012), pp. 219–224

19. J. Szefer, R.B. Lee, A case for hardware protection of guest VMS from compromised hypervisors in cloud computing, in *2011 31st International Conference on Distributed Computing Systems Workshops (ICDCSW)* (IEEE, New York, 2011), pp. 248–252

20. D. Perez-Botero, J. Szefer, R.B. Lee, Characterizing hypervisor vulnerabilities in cloud computing servers, in *Proceedings of the 2013 International Workshop on Security in Cloud Computing* (ACM, New York, 2013), pp. 3–10

21. V. Varadarajan, T. Kooburat, B. Farley, T. Ristenpart, M.M. Swift, Resource-freeing attacks: improve your cloud performance (at your neighbor's expense), in *Proceedings of the 2012 ACM Conference on Computer and Communications Security* (ACM, New York, 2012), pp. 281–292

22. Y. Zhou, D. Feng, Side-channel attacks: Ten years after its publication and the impacts on cryptographic module security testing. IACR Cryptol. ePrint Arch. **2005**, 388 (2005)

23. Y. Zhang, A. Juels, A. Oprea, M.K. Reiter, *Homealone: Co-residency detection in the cloud via side-channel analysis, in 2011 IEEE Symposium on Security and Privacy (SP)* (IEEE, New York, 2011), pp. 313–328

24. Y. Xu, M. Bailey, F. Jahanian, K. Joshi, M. Hiltunen, R. Schlichting, An exploration of l2 cache covert channels in virtualized environments, in *Proceedings of the 3rd ACM workshop on Cloud Computing Security Workshop* (ACM, New York, 2011), pp. 29–40

25. M. Weiß, B. Heinz, F. Stumpf, *A cache timing attack on aes in virtualization environments, in Financial Cryptography and Data Security* (Springer, Heidelberg, 2012), pp. 314–328

26. A. Aviram, S. Hu, B. Ford, R. Gummadi, Determinating timing channels in compute clouds, in *Proceedings of the 2010 ACM Workshop on Cloud Computing Security Workshop* (ACM, New York, 2010), pp. 103–108

27. R. Martin, J. Demme, S. Sethumadhavan, Timewarp: rethinking timekeeping and performance monitoring mechanisms to mitigate side-channel attacks. ACM SIGARCH Comput. Architect. News **40**(3), 118–129 (2012)

28. J. Shi, X. Song, H. Chen, B. Zang, Limiting cache-based side-channel in multi-tenant cloud using dynamic page coloring, in *2011 IEEE/IFIP 41st International Conference on Dependable Systems and Networks Workshops (DSN-W)* (IEEE, New York, 2011), pp. 194–199

29. T. Kim, M. Peinado, G. Mainar-Ruiz, Stealthmem: system-level protection against cache-based side channel attacks in the cloud, in *Presented as part of the 21st USENIX Security Symposium (USENIX Security 12)* (2012), pp. 189–204

30. B. Sevak, Security against side channel attack in cloud computing. Int. J. Eng. Adv. Technol. (IJEAT) **2**(2), 183 (2013)

31. D. Stefan, P. Buiras, E.Z. Yang, A. Levy, D. Terei, A. Russo, D. Mazières, *Eliminating cache-based timing attacks with instruction-based scheduling, in Computer Security-ESORICS 2013* (Springer, Heidelberg, 2013), pp. 718–735

32. B.C. Vattikonda, S. Das, H. Shacham, Eliminating fine grained timers in xen, in *Proceedings of the 3rd ACM Workshop on Cloud Computing Security Workshop* (ACM, New York, 2011), pp. 41–46

33. Y. Zhang, M. Li, K. Bai, M. Yu, W. Zang, *Incentive compatible moving target defense against VM-colocation attacks in clouds, in Information Security and Privacy Research* (Springer, Heidelberg, 2012), pp. 388–399

34. M. Godfrey, M. Zulkernine, A server-side solution to cache-based side-channel attacks in the cloud, in *2013 IEEE Sixth International Conference on Cloud Computing* (IEEE, New York, 2013), pp. 163–170

35. A.C. Atici, C. Yilmaz, E. Savas, An approach for isolating the sources of information leakage exploited in cache-based side-channel attacks, in *2013 IEEE 7th International Conference on Software Security and Reliability-Companion (SERE-C)* (IEEE, New York, 2013), pp. 74–83

36. T. Ristenpart, E. Tromer, H. Shacham, S. Savage, Hey, you, get off of my cloud: exploring information leakage in third-party compute clouds, in *Proceedings of the 16th ACM Conference on Computer and Communications Security* (ACM, New York, 2009), pp. 199–212

37. Y. Zhang, A. Juels, M.K. Reiter, T. Ristenpart, Cross-VM side channels and their use to extract private keys, in *Proceedings of the 2012 ACM Conference on Computer and Communications Security* (ACM, New York, 2012), pp. 305–316

38. T. ElGamal, *A public key cryptosystem and a signature scheme based on discrete logarithms, in Advances in Cryptology* (Springer, Heidelberg, 1984), pp. 10–18

39. T. Elgamal, A public key cryptosystem and a signature scheme based on discrete logarithms. IEEE Trans. Inf. Theor. **31**(4), 469–472 (1985)

40. S.J. Stolfo, M.B. Salem, A.D. Keromytis, *Fog computing: Mitigating insider data theft attacks in the cloud, in 2012 IEEE Symposium on Security and Privacy Workshops (SPW)* (IEEE, New York, 2012), pp. 125–128

41. I.D.C.L. Ayala, M. Vega, M. Vargas-Lombardo, *Emerging threats, risk and attacks in distributed systems: cloud computing, in Innovations and Advances in Computer, Information, Systems Sciences, and Engineering* (Springer, Heidelberg, 2013), pp. 37–51

42. V. Varadharajan, U. Tupakula, Counteracting security attacks in virtual machines in the cloud using property based attestation. J. Netw. Comput. Appl. **40**, 31–45 (2014)

43. T.H. Noor, Q.Z. Sheng, A. Alfazi, *Detecting occasional reputation attacks on cloud services, in Web Engineering* (Springer, Heidelberg, 2013), pp. 416–423

44. A. Patel, M. Taghavi, K. Bakhtiyari, J.C. Júnior, An intrusion detection and prevention system in cloud computing: a systematic review. J. Netw. Comput. Appl. **36**(1), 25–41 (2013)

45. T.H. Noor, Q.Z. Sheng, S. Zeadally, J. Yu, Trust management of services in cloud environments: obstacles and solutions. ACM Comput. Surv. (CSUR) **46**(1), 12 (2013)

46. R. Bhadauria, S. Sanyal, Survey on security issues in cloud computing and associated mitigation techniques (2012), arXiv preprint arXiv:1204.0764

Chapter 5
General Cloud Security Recommendations

Abstract This short chapter introduces a general list of recommendations for enhancing cloud security.

Keywords Cloud computing · IaaS · PaaS · SaaS · Cloud security · Cloud recommendations

5.1 Introduction

As we have discussed in the earlier chapters, cloud security can be overwhelming. Many security aspects need to be covered to get to the point where cloud usage is safe and efficient. Although security becomes more complex when creating your own private cloud, some organizations are obligated to use private clouds for reasons related to governance and data ownership.

Generally, private clouds are more suitable for large organizations with adequate resources. For small and medium businesses, a public or community cloud might be the answer. As explained in the previous chapters, public clouds come with a longer list of threats as compared to private clouds. However, in most cases, private clouds are out of the question because of financial implication.

The different service models and operational cost savings make the cloud a very appealing choice. In 2013, a survey was conducted that included 1000 small- and medium-sized businesses. The survey found that the businesses that adopted Cloud technologies were twice as likely to see an earnings uplift in the year before [1]. The survey also found that only 16 % of the participating businesses were using cloud computing and 38 % have a business website.

Another study was published in 2013 analyzed businesses in Australia and concluded that small- and medium-sized businesses were losing 24$ billion annually due to bad IT management [2]. The study found that nontechnical IT managers spend an average of 3.1 h/week handling IT management issues instead of attending their day-to-day duties. The study suggested that performance would greatly improve if these small- to medium-sized businesses embrace the cloud as their IT solution.

M.M. Alani, *Elements of Cloud Computing Security*,
SpringerBriefs in Computer Science, DOI 10.1007/978-3-319-41411-9_5

Despite of all what we have mentioned, moving to the cloud is not an easy decision. Many choices need to be made to land the most suitable solution for the organization. Security remains the major concern for all cloud computing adopters and an important deciding factor.

5.2 General Security Recommendations

The following list provides general recommendation for cloud computing security:

- Install and maintain a firewall configuration.
  A firewall should be placed at each external network interface and between each security zone within the cloud [3]. This would assure that all ingress and egress traffic is being filtered. However, firewall rules should be written carefully so as not to allow unwanted traffic and close all unused ports. In [4], a general framework of cloud firewall was suggested. The proposed framework features event-level detection chain with dynamic resource allocation. The mathematical model for the proposed framework was also introduced. Moreover, a linear resource investment function was proposed for economical dynamical resource allocation for cloud firewalls.
- Do not use vendor-supplied defaults for passwords and other security parameters.
  The default usernames, passwords, and other security parameters are well known to other cloud users, and probably many outsiders. It is vital the first step done when you receive your account credentials that you change passwords for all accounts.
- Research into standardized SLAs and liability provisions could lead to greater accountability [5].
  SLAs are important documents that govern the client's relationship with the cloud service provider. Its an important step to research standardized SLAs and check the SLA you are about to sign very well before signing. Any deviation from the standardized SLA needs to be thoroughly explained to you by the cloud service provider. SLAs define the line that separates the service provider's duties from the client's duties.
- Do not setup your own cloud unless it is necessary.
  Scenarios where the organization decides to build its own private cloud have to be limited all of the following conditions:

  1. The organization is obliged by some governance laws or guidelines that force them to host their user data inside their premises.
  2. The organization has adequate budget for the project. As we have explained in Chap. 1, the capital expenditures for starting a private cloud are very high.
  3. In the case that the organization, for security purposes, intends to build their private cloud, they will have to provide the human resources needed for the job. In some looser scenarios, it would be possible for the organization to outsource the creation of the cloud and be responsible for cloud maintenance only. In that

case, the organization must have the human resources capable of maintaining the cloud.

4. The organization must be capable of creating and maintaining a proper incident response plan, disaster recovery plan, and business continuity plan, along with all their requirements (e.g., backup generators, backup Internet connection, alternate location, etc.)

Unless all of the aforementioned conditions exist, it is recommended that the organization considers public cloud service providers or alternative solutions such as community cloud, or even a hybrid cloud solution.

- Ensure that no unnecessary functions or processes are active.

  When unnecessary processes or functions are active, it is highly probable that these processes or functions have open ports on the firewall side. When you run unnecessary processes, you are broadening the range of threats with an unnecessary exposure to vulnerabilities in processes and functions that you do not even need. In many operating systems, the list of services and processes enabled by default can be very long.

- Ensure patch management.

  Security vulnerabilities are detected every day. It is important to keep all the systems patched in a timely manner. This should be assured at the host-machine level and the guest-machine level. In the recent years, attention has been given to a class of attacks called zero-day attacks. A zero-day attack is an attack which exploit vulnerabilities that have not been disclosed publicly [6]. Methods of defense against these attacks are not available until they are detected publicly. Among the findings that [6] presented are given below:

1. Zero-day attacks are more frequent than previously thought: 11 out of 18 vulnerabilities identified were not known zero-day vulnerabilities.
2. Zero-day attacks last between 19 days and 30 months, with a median of 8 months and an average of approximately 10 months.
3. After zero-day vulnerabilities are disclosed, the number of malware variants exploiting them increases 18385,000 times and the number of attacks increases 2100,000 times.
4. Exploits for 42 % of all vulnerabilities employed in host-based threats are detected in field data within 30 days after the disclosure date.

These findings tell us how important it is to keep all our systems patched and updated. Keep in mind that these findings are for the years 2008–2011. However, they give us a general idea of how bad zero-day attacks are. As there is not much to do in defense from zero-day attacks, patching in a timely manner is important. The security personnel in the organization need to be up to date on all new vulnerabilities, threats, and attacks.

- Protect encryption keys from misuse or disclosure.

  In one way or another, encryption is a necessity on the cloud. We have discussed the different mitigation techniques to thwart threats to confidentiality in Chap. 3

so we are not going to discuss them here. However, we need to emphasize the importance of safeguarding the encryption keys.

- Promptly revoke access for terminated users [3].
  When an employee is no longer affiliated with the organization, it is very important that that employees credentials are removed from the system, or at least disabled. A disgruntled former employee can cause harm by misusing the privileges that were not revoked in a timely manner. This also applies to temporary accounts created for guests or partners as well.

More general discussions and recommendations about cloud security can be found in [7–11].

References

1. H. Osman, Smbs that embrace cloud enjoy more revenue: Myob, http://goo.gl/nRMsK0. Accessed 03 April 2016
2. T. Bindi, Smbs losing billions due to ineffective it management, http://www.dynamicbusiness. com.au/news/smbs-losing-billions-due-to-ineffective-it-management-24042013.html. Accessed 03 April 2016
3. A. Buecker, K. Lodewijkx, H. Moss, K. Skapinetz, M. Waidner, Cloud security guidance ibm recommendations for the implementation of cloud security. IBM Redpaper (2009)
4. S. Yu, R. Doss, W. Zhou, S. Guo, A general cloud firewall framework with dynamic resource allocation, in *2013 IEEE International Conference on Communications (ICC)* (IEEE, New York, 2013), pp. 1941–1945
5. N. Robinson, L. Valeri, J. Cave, T. Starkey, H. Graux, S. Creese, P. Hopkins, The cloud: understanding the security, privacy and trust challenges. Rand Corporation (2011)
6. L. Bilge, T. Dumitras, Before we knew it: an empirical study of zero-day attacks in the real world, in *Proceedings of the 2012 ACM Conference on Computer and Communications Security*, (ACM, New York, 2012), pp. 833–844
7. L. Wei, H. Zhu, Z. Cao, X. Dong, W. Jia, Y. Chen, A.V. Vasilakos, Security and privacy for storage and computation in cloud computing. Inf. Sci. **258**, 371–386 (2014)
8. X. He, T. Chomsiri, P. Nanda, Z. Tan, Improving cloud network security using the tree-rule firewall. Future Gener. Comput. Syst. **30**, 116–126 (2014)
9. S. Koushik, A.P. Patil, Open security system for cloud architecture, in *ICT and Critical Infrastructure: Proceedings of the 48th Annual Convention of Computer Society of India*, vol I (Springer, Heidelberg, 2014), pp. 467–471
10. V.J. Winkler, *Securing the Cloud: Cloud Computer Security Techniques and Tactics* (Elsevier, Amsterdam, 2011)
11. H. Xiangyi, M. Zhanguo, L. Yu, The research of the cloud security architecture, in *Instrumentation, Measurement, Circuits and Systems* (Springer, Heidelberg, 2012), pp. 379–385

Index

A
Amazon Web Services (AWS), 3
Application Programming Interface
 (API), 9
Attack, 41
Attribute Based Encryption (ABE), 27

C
Cloud infrastructure, 7
CloudFlare, 19
Clustering, 5
Collusion attack, 27
Community cloud, 12
Cross-Site Scripting (XSS), 22

D
Denial of Service (DoS), 30, 41
Distributed Denial of Service (DDoS), 18,
 42

F
Fraudulent Resource Consumption (FRC),
 17

H
HTTPS, 22
Hybrid cloud, 12
Hypervisor, 7, 44

P
Private cloud, 11
Public cloud, 11

R
Resource Freeing Attack (RFA), 45

S
Secure Socket Layer (SSL), 22
Security Educations, Training, and Aware-
 ness (SETA), 29
Service Level Agreement (SLA), 36, 52
Side-Channel Attack, 46
Software-Defined Network (SDN), 44
Spamhaus, 19
Spear-phishing, 21, 28
Spoofing, 19

T
Threat, 25
Transport Layer Security (TLS), 22

V
Virtual Private Server (VPS), 2

W
World Wide Web (WWW), 1

© The Author(s) 2016
M.M. Alani, *Elements of Cloud Computing Security*,
SpringerBriefs in Computer Science, DOI 10.1007/978-3-319-41411-9

Printed in the United States
By Bookmasters